JG 54

A Photographic History of the Grunherzjäger

JG 54

A Photographic History of the Grunherzjäger

Werner Held/Hannes Trautloft/
Ekkehard Bob

Translated from the German by Don Cox

Schiffer Military/Aviation History
Atglen, PA

Dust jacket artwork by Steve Ferguson, Colorado Springs, CO

THE HEART THEY LEFT BEHIND

The combat scene is of I/JG 54s Otto Kittel in his Fw 190 A-6 "White 1" – with the calico camouflage, typical of Grunherz aircraft in late 1943 – just after he has knocked down a pair of Yak-9s. In the subsequent winter retreat to the west, I/JG 54 once again white-washed their Fw 190s, and likewise abandoned most of their unit markings. Throughout 1944, they opted for a variety of heavy earth-tone camouflage schemes which often omitted or overpainted Staffel numbers. During the fierce winter of 1944-1945, Staffelkapitän Otto Kittel was still overshadowed by the accomplishments of his brethren in the west, but "the heart they left behind" in Russia accounted for his 267th aerial victory before he was lost in combat on February 15, 1945. At the time, few knew Kittel had become the fourth leading fighter ace of all time.

Translated from the German by Don Cox.

Library of Congress Catalog Number: 94-66969

This book was originally published under the title,
Die Grunherzjäger, Bildchronik des Jagdgeschwaders 54,
by Podzun-Pallas Verlag, Friedberg.

Printed in the United States of America.
ISBN: 0-88740-690-4

Contents

Introduction

This book is the story of Jagdgeschwader 54's operations during the Second World War. The Geschwader was one of the twelve Jagdgeschwader of the Luftwaffe which formed the basis of the German day fighter force at the outbreak of the war. It saw action in nearly every European theater of combat. Despite the fact that the Geschwader's airfields were often scattered over vast areas of the front plus the role that frequent change and relocation played in the affairs of the Geschwader – at times giving the appearance of fragmenting the unit – neither the incessant turnover of commanders in each unit nor death itself, striking with its lightning fury, could damage the integrity of the Geschwader.

With over 9,400 air victories to its credit, Jagdgeschwader 54 is numbered among the most successful units of the German Luftwaffe.

This volume is a result of a cooperative effort between former members of the Geschwader and Werner Held. For this, our thanks go out to all who provided assistance.

The pages of this uncompromising photo documentation mirror the path and life of Jagdgeschwader 54 with all its peaks and valleys. This portrayal does not lay claim to revealing the history of Jagdgeschwader 54 in its most minute details, as can be found in a "Geschwader journal."

But at the same time this book is also much more than a mere "family album." It brings back memories of the lives of victorious pilots and of the men who, by their quiet and dedicated work on the ground, made the unique success of the Geschwader possible in the first place.

These photos give an impressive account of work and mission operations – and how the feelings of joy and pain in the Geschwader were inexorably tied together. What they cannot show, however, is the lonely deaths of our pilots in the cockpits of their planes. The spirit of the old Geschwader and the men who immortalized that spirit are brought to life once again when viewing these photos.

During the course of the war Jagdgeschwader 54 was known as the "Grünherzgeschwader" – the "Green Heart Geschwader." As a visible sign of the Geschwader's unity, all aircraft and vehicles wore the Geschwader's coat-of-arms – a large green heart which encompassed the coats-of-arms of the subordinate Jagdgruppen inspired by the heritage of our countrymen. This "green heart" is a symbol of my Thuringian homeland, to which I feel very close ties. At the time, no one could have guessed that this symbol would have a particularly special meaning in our day – namely as a way to strike a bridge of unity and maintain a constant reminder to the people on the other side of a divisive and inhuman border, in the non-free green heart of Germany.

Only five years elapsed from the time the Geschwader was established in Hechingen, at the foot of the Hohenzollernburg, on 1 February 1940 until its disbandment in May of 1945 in Schleswig-Holstein. A short period of time from an historical perspective, to be sure, but to the men of the Geschwader, it was a long, bitter period of privation.

Nevertheless, this time period was sufficient enough to develop a large and inseparable family, to cultivate an unshakable union of pilots and soldiers out of a "heap" of men haphazardly thrown together. Anyone who couldn't fit into this family separated himself quickly and painlessly, like a biological foreign body.

The common experience shared in Jagdgeschwader 54 during the war has kept alive a mutual association of a growing camaraderie –despite all the confusion and distractions which have occurred in the postwar period. Now, 40 years later, no one asks anymore who was once an officer, an NCO, or a private. Nor does it make a difference if the person was a minister, professor, doctor, journalist, artist, official, or factory worker after the war.

An explanatory section on the Grünherzgeschwader is provided, both as a general clarification and to provide the reader and viewer having little or no comprehension of fighter operations a better understanding of the pictures. This includes the Geschwader's birth, organization, missions, successes, losses, and information about its personnel.

All official war journals of the Grünherzgeschwader have disappeared. Only a few private notes by former members of the Geschwader were available for the text of this photo chronicle. A faultless chronology is not always possible after 40 years – particularly with reference to specific dates, positions of authority, names of operational airfields, or persons appearing in the photos. Small imperfections must therefore be tolerated.

We Grünherz fighters had eyes that could see what was happening during those times, yet we were bound by duty and an oath to endure the struggle to its bitter end.

At that time, we believed in doing our best for the Fatherland in fulfilling this oath. In doing so, we relied upon our own strength.

Our Geschwader can count upon a heritage of bravery with which its men fought, a sense of fairness and decency with regard to the enemy, and above all, a rejection of despicable and shameful acts behind the front lines carried out against a defenseless minority among our people.

Who would accuse us because we held fast, because we had no desire to see our ground troops die, caught in hopeless situations lying in the muck, or watch our wives and children perish in a hailstorm of bombs?

To be sure, during those difficult times there were also moments of inner and outer crises, moments when our nerves had been stretched to the breaking point, moments where we doubted if anything made sense anymore.

However, no one can argue the legitimacy of our actions. We made truly great sacrifices for it.

Those who experienced the horrors of war, who knew what it meant to fear for one's own life, and yet who overcame all these weaknesses and flew into the defending fire, these were they who learned to hate the war.

We survivors of the Grünherzgeschwader can therefore only warn against another horrible repetition.

But what soldier is ever asked whether or not he wants to fight?

Which soldier is allowed to make the decision whether or not he prefers to work in the employ of this government or that government?

Our dead comrades from the Grünherzgeschwader, to whom this book is dedicated, are an admonishment and a continual reminder to us that the deaths of millions of people could only possibly serve a purpose if it would enable mankind to finally realize that wars are the most wasteful and inhumane means to resolve conflicts between peoples.

It is only possible to avoid war, however, by him who is truly prepared to defend his country. We can therefore only hope that our country will continue to live in peace and not be called upon to defend our freedoms.

Following the war, it was the pilots of all nations who were the first to extend a reconciliatory hand to their former enemies. They are also those today whose visions extend beyond all borders and who search for unity in a world caught up in change, in a world whose statesmen must seriously strive toward peace. We old "Grünherz" fighters stand arm in arm with them in these efforts.

Hannes Trautloft

Listing of the Most Important Airfields and Sites

Deutschland: (Nr. 35 – 87)

- Achmer (39)
- Bad Zwischenahn
- Bissel
- Blumenfeld (84)
- Böblingen (69)
- Cloppenburg
- Dedelsdorf
- Delmenhorst (44)
- Devau
- Dortmund (37)
- Eutingen (Horb) (67)
- Flensburg (57)
- Frankfurt (Main) (61)
- Friedrichshafen (70)
- Fürstenau (42)
- Gardelegen (59)
- Gelnhausen (62)
- Gerlinden (87)
- Großenhain (64)
- Güstrow
- Gutenfeld (80)
- Hechingen (68)
- Heiligenbeil (77)
- Herzogenaurach (73)
- Hesepe
- Hopsten
- Illesheim (Aisch) (72)
- Insterburg (82)
- Jagel
- Jesau
- Jever (48)
- Kiel (56)
- Klein-Kummersfelde
- Köln-Butzweilerhof (35)
- Königsberg (79)
- Krefeld (36)
- Landau (Isar) (74)
- Liegnitz (66)
- Lindental (86)
- Löbnitz
- Ludwigslust (51)
- Lübeck (53)
- Lüneburg (50)
- Marienburg (76)
- Memmingen (71)
- Mönchengladbach
- Mörtitz
- Münster-Handorf (38)
- Neuhausen (81)
- Neukuhren (78)
- Neumünster
- Ober-Olm (60)
- Odderade (54)
- Oldenburg (45)
- Pillau
- Plantlünne (40)
- Prenzlau
- Rautenberg
- Rheine
- Rogau-Rosenau
- Rostken (83)
- Rotenburg (b. Bremen) (49)
- Sagan (65)
- Schleswig (55)
- Schwerin (52)
- Stolp (Pommern) (75)
- Süderhastedt
- Trakehnen (85)
- Varrelbusch (43)
- Vörden (41)
- Walldorf
- Wesermünde
- Westerland (58)
- Zella-Mehlis (63)

Belgien: (Nr. 21 – 22)

- Brüssel (22)
- Gent–St. Denis (21)
- Neuchâteau
- Peer

Finnland: (Nr. 165 – 168)

- Helsinki (165)
- Immola (166)
- Petäjarvi (168)
- Viipuri (167)

Frankreich: (Nr. 1 – 20)

- Aumale
- Auffains
- Beaulieu
- Bergerac (4)
- Biarritz (2)
- Cambrai (16)
- Campagne (19)
- Cazaux (3)
- Châteaudun (Orleans)
- Cherbourg (11)
- Conteville
- Evreux (9)
- Guines (19)
- Guise (14)
- Harlinghem (20)
- Hirson (Beaulieu) (15)
- Laval (7)
- Le Mans (6)
- Lille-Bendeville (17)
- Monchy-Breton (St. Pol)
- Norrent-Fontes
- Orleans (5)
- Paris-Orly (12)
- Poix
- Rouen (10)
- Toulouse (1)
- Villa Coubly (Paris) (8)
- Vitry en Artois (13)
- Yvrench

Holland: (Nr. 23 – 34)

- Arnheim (27)
- Bergen (NH) (am Zee) (32)
- Deelen (28)
- De Kooi (NH) (am Zee) (33)
- Eindhoven (26)
- Groningen (34)
- Hamstede (24)
- Katwijk (29)
- Schipohl-Amsterdam (31)
- Soesterberg (30)
- Vlissingen (23)
- Waalhaven (25)

Jugoslawien: (Nr. 92 – 94)

- Belgrad-Semlin (93)
- Bijeljina (94)
- Pancevo (92)

Österreich: (Nr. 88 – 91)

- Graz (91)
- Parndorf (90)
- Salzburg (88)
- Wien-Aspern (89)

Polen: (Nr. 100 – 108)

- Bialystok (106)
- Camiey-Radom (102)
- Deblin (103)
- Lemberg (100)
- Lublin (101)
- Modlin (104)
- Nasielsk (105)
- Pultusk (107)
- Wottkowicc
- Zichenau (108)

Rumänien: (Nr. 95 – 99)

- Arad (95)
- Detta (96)
- Leipzig (Bessarabien) (98)
- Mamaia (Konstanza) (99)
- Roman (97)

Sowjetunion: (Nr.109 – 164)

- Baranowitschi (152)
- Birzi (Jakobstadt) (112)
- Bobruisk (153)
- Bol. Rudka
- Bol. Wischera
- Briansk (154)
- Charkow (160)
- Chatalowka (161)
- Cholm (142)
- Cirava (116)
- Corosowo
- Demjansk (141)
- Dno (139)
- Dorpat (124)
- Dugino (145)
- Dünaburg (111)
- Gatschina (132)
- Gdow (130)
- Idriza (143)
- Isotscha
- Iwanowka (164)
- Jakobstadt (112)
- Karatschew (155)
- Kedainiai (109)
- Kiew (159)
- Korovje-Selo
- Kotly (131)
- Krasnogwardeisk (Gatschina) (132)
- Kursk (157)
- Libau-Grobin (114)
- Lissino
- Ljuban (135)
- Luga
- Mal-Owsischtschi (Samra-See)
- Mga (134)
- Minsk (151)
- Narwa (129)
- Nikolskoje
- Ösel (Insel) (126)
- Orel (156)
- Orscha (150)
- Ostrow (121)
- Pankowo
- Pernau (126)
- Petseri
- Pleskau (122)
- Polosk (148)
- Poltawa (162)
- Porchow (123)
- Reval (127)
- Riga (113)
- Rjelbitzi (138)
- Robty
- Roskopolje
- Rshew (144)
- Sarudinje
- Schaplino
- Schatalowka
- Schaulen (110)
- Schwanenburg (120)
- Shitomir (158)
- Siwerskaja (133)
- Skirotava (Riga) (113)
- Skundra (118)
- Smolensk (149)
- Staraja-Russa (140)
- Szoltzy (137)
- Tessowo (136)
- Torma
- Torrossowo
- Tukum (119)
- Tuleblja
- Wereteni
- Wesenberg (128)
- Windau (115)
- Winniza (163)
- Witebsk (147)
- Wjasma (146)
- Zabeln (117)

Ungarn: (Nr. 91)

- Fünfkirchen (91)

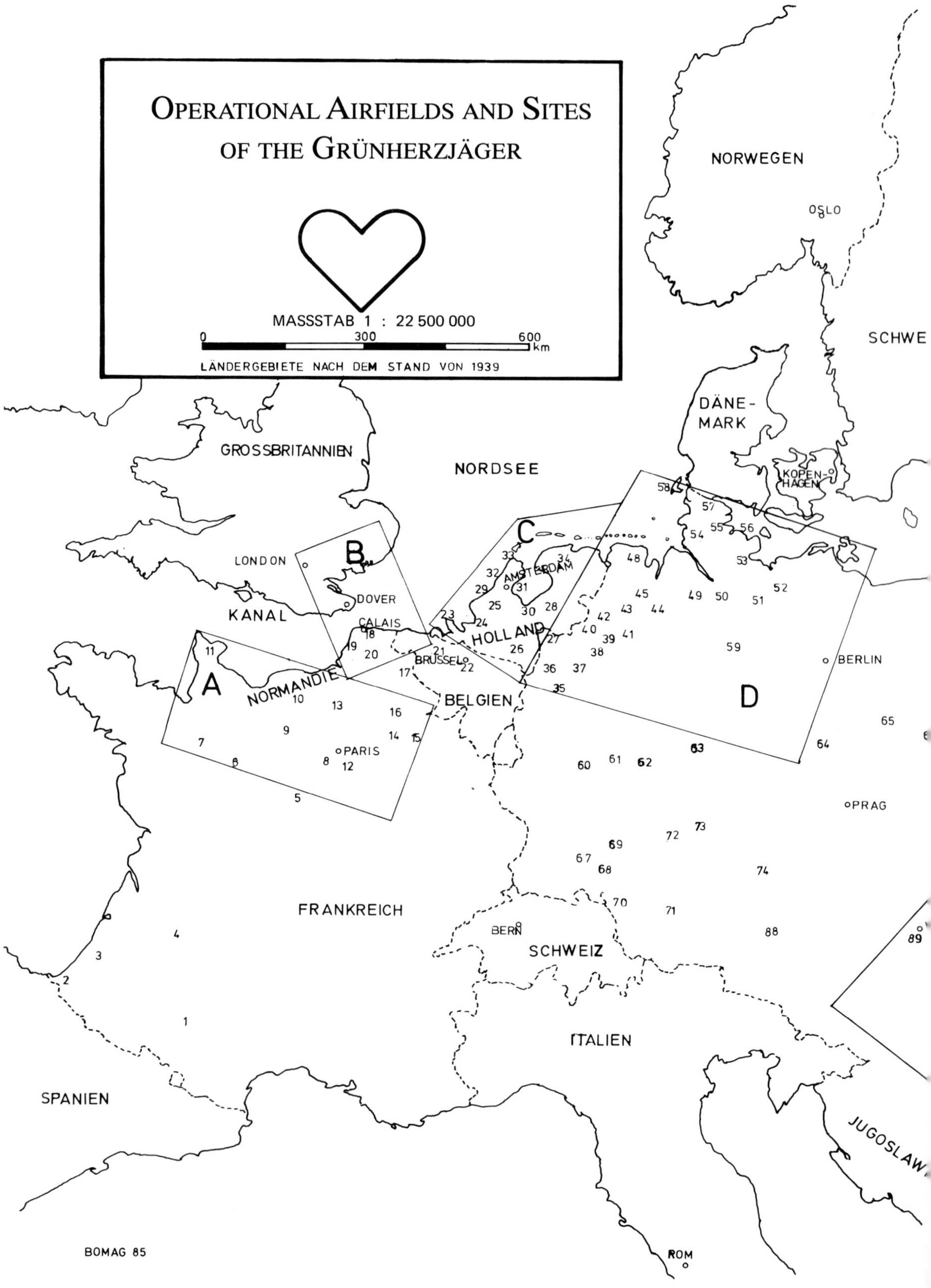
OPERATIONAL AIRFIELDS AND SITES OF THE GRÜNHERZJÄGER
MASSSTAB 1 : 22 500 000
0 300 600 km
LÄNDERGEBIETE NACH DEM STAND VON 1939
NORWEGEN
OSLO
SCHWE
DÄNE-MARK
KOPEN-HAGEN
GROSSBRITANNIEN
NORDSEE
LONDON
DOVER
KANAL
CALAIS
NORMANDIE
BRÜSSEL
HOLLAND
AMSTERDAM
BELGIEN
BERLIN
PARIS
PRAG
FRANKREICH
BERN
SCHWEIZ
ITALIEN
SPANIEN
JUGOSLAW
ROM
A
B
C
D
BOMAG 85

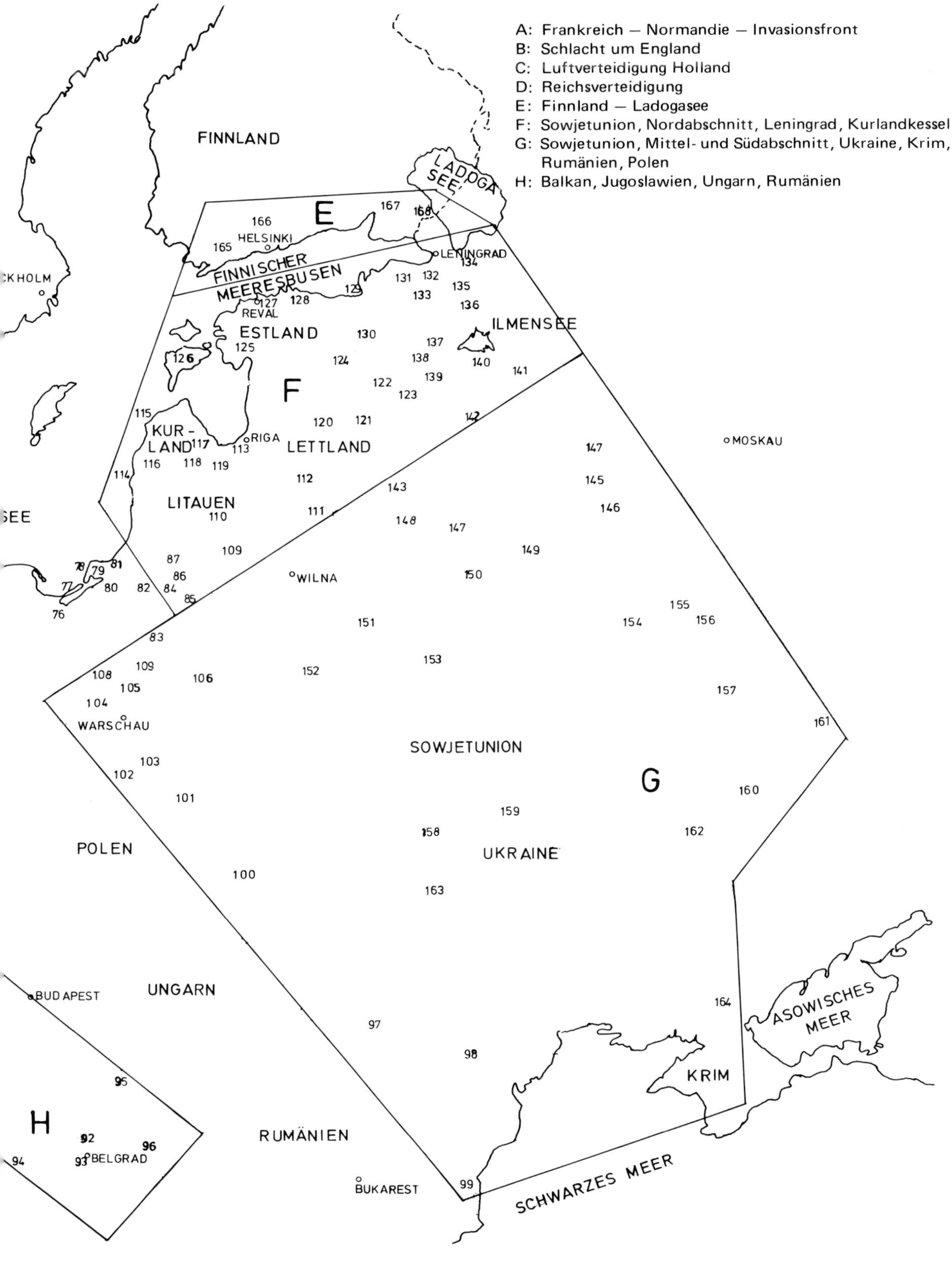
A: Frankreich — Normandie — Invasionsfront
B: Schlacht um England
C: Luftverteidigung Holland
D: Reichsverteidigung
E: Finnland — Ladogasee
F: Sowjetunion, Nordabschnitt, Leningrad, Kurlandkessel
G: Sowjetunion, Mittel- und Südabschnitt, Ukraine, Krim, Rumänien, Polen
H: Balkan, Jugoslawien, Ungarn, Rumänien
FINNLAND
LADOGA SEE
E
HELSINKI
LENINGRAD
FINNISCHER MEERESBUSEN
REVAL
ESTLAND
ILMENSEE
F
KUR-LAND
RIGA
LETTLAND
MOSKAU
LITAUEN
WILNA
WARSCHAU
SOWJETUNION
G
POLEN
UKRAINE
UNGARN
BUDAPEST
ASOWISCHES MEER
KRIM
H
BELGRAD
RUMÄNIEN
BUKAREST
SCHWARZES MEER

Organization of the Grünherzgeschwader

The following units were subordinate to the Geschwader headquarters unit of Jagdgeschwader 54 (Stab JG 54):

I Jagdgruppe (I/JG 54)
II Jagdgruppe (II/JG 54)
III Jagdgruppe (III/JG 54)
IV Jagdgruppe (IV/JG 54)
Ergänzungsjagdstaffel (E/JG 54)

The Geschwader size corresponded roughly to that of a regiment in the German Army. Total personnel strength varied between 2,200 and 2,800 officers, clerks, NCOs, and lower ranking enlisted. Of these, 120 to 160 were pilots, with the rest of the personnel carrying out the numerous ground duties.

The Geschwaderstab

The Geschwaderkommodore (an Oberst) commanded the Geschwader both in the air and on the ground. He was assisted in his leadership responsibilities on the ground by a Geschwaderadjutant (an Oberleutnant or Hauptmann), the Ia, who was at the same time the Major im Stabe, the Technischer Offizier (technical officer, an Oberleutnant/Hauptmann), the Kraftfahroffizier (motor pool officer, a Leutnant/Oberleutnant), the Nachrichtenoffizier (communications officer, an Oberleutnant/Hauptmann), and finally, an administration clerk.

In addition to these officers there was also a lower staff with 50 to 60 NCOs and enlisted ranks, consisting of staff secretaries, vehicle drivers, general troop administrative personnel, plus a group of maintenance personnel to keep the four HQ aircraft serviceable.

A Luftnachrichtenkompanie (air communications company) was also subordinate to the Geschwaderstab. This was under the command of an Oberleutnant or Hauptmann (at the same time the Geschwadernachrichtenoffizier. The Luftnachrichtenkompanie was organized into a Funkzug (radio platoon), a Fernsprechbauzug (communications setup platoon) and a Luftnachrichten-Betriebszug (communications operations platoon). Including the general administrative personnel, the Luftnachrichtenkompanie had a total strength of approximately 150 soldiers.

A **Jagdgruppe** corresponded in size to an Army battalion. It consisted of a Gruppenstab, a Stabskompanie, and three Jagdstaffeln (sometimes increased to four during the course of the war).

The structure of the Gruppenstab was similar to the Geschwaderstab. The Gruppenkommandeur was a Hauptmann or Major, who led his Gruppe both on the ground and in the air. He was supported in his ground duties by a Gruppenadjutant (Leutnant/Oberleutnant), the Hauptmann beim Stab, the Technischer Offizier (Leutnant/Oberleutnant), the Nachrichtenoffizier (Leutnant/Oberleutnant), the Chef der Stabskompanie (Hauptmann), the Gruppe's flight surgeon, two administrative clerks, and a weapons maintenance official.

The Stabsschwarm of the Jagdgruppe consisted of four fighter aircraft.

The Stabskompanie was tasked with carrying out major repairs and maintenance work on aircraft and vehicles as well as on the heavy equipment of the Jagdgruppe. It comprised 260 NCOs and enlisted personnel.

The Stabskompanie was organized into a Werftzug (maintenance platoon), Nachrichtenzug (communications platoon), and Kraftfahrzeugzug (motor pool). The Flakzug (anti-aircraft platoon) for airfield protection, along with other personnel, were also subordinate to the Stabskompanie.

Total strength of a Jagdgruppe varied between 600 and 800 officers, clerks, NCOs, and enlisted.

A **Jagdstaffel** was commanded by a Staffelkapitän (Leutnant/Oberleutnant/Hauptmann) both in the air and on the ground. It corresponded to an Army company. As a rule, 12 pilots belonged to a Staffel, of which two to four were flying Staffel officers (Leutnante/ Oberleutnante). The Jagdstaffel consisted of 110 officers, NCOs, and enlisted, of which 98 were ground support personnel.

The **Ergänzungsstaffel** was organized in a similar fashion to a normal Jagdstaffel with regards to personnel and equipment. It was commanded by an Oberleutnant or Hauptmann. Several fighter pilot instructors were provided for training the young pilots fresh from school.

The Geschwader's Gruppen – often even individual Staffeln – were generally dispersed at different airfield sites, sometimes separated from each other by great distances.

The Grünherz Pilots

The pilots of the Grünherzgeschwader came from all points of the compass of our Fatherland; many dialects could be heard in their ranks. In addition to the active career officers and NCOs, numerous reservists also flew in the individual Staffeln. Many of the Grünherz fighters came from craftsmen and technical trades, which, because of their young ages, they had often had only practiced for a short time. But among these pilots there were also the sons of farmers, butchers, bakers, barbers, community officials, clerks, musicians and goldsmiths. A large number of these young pilots came to the Grünherzgeschwader as students directly from the classroom or lecture hall. The weight of the fight rested upon the shoulders of youth, those special youth who carried out their duties as pilot, Staffel commander, Kommandeur and Kommodore far beyond the maturity of their years.

The ages of the pilots varied between 19 and 31 years. The majority – and the highest scoring as well – were in the age group between 22 and 28 years old.

The ranks of the pilots ranged from Gefreiter to Major.

A Jagdgruppe with three Staffeln normally had 40 pilots, later 52 and more with four Staffeln; of these, 16 to 20 were officers and the remaining pilots were of NCO ranks.

The flying personnel of the Grünherzgeschwader fluctuated between 120 to 180 pilots.

Following flight basic training, fighter pilot recruits went through a special fighter pilot training course at the fighter pilot schools (Jagdfliegerschulen). The final education of these young flyers, however, took place in the Geschwader's Ergänzungsstaffel. It was there that they were prepared for their upcoming front-line operations in the Grünherzgeschwader.

Numerous NCOs pilots in the Grünherzgeschwader were given field commissions due to their high number of air victories and the bravery they exhibited in the face of the enemy. Many of these later led their own Staffeln and, in rarer cases, even Jagdgruppen.

Included among the pilots in the Grünherzgeschwader were wiry, fresh, lively ladder-climbers – possessed by an unbridled will of attack, wit, humor, a quick retort, quick-mind, and a spirit of independence.

Their gear was determined by the particular front they were fighting on and the season. In the Battle of Britain and during flights over the Channel, and later over the North Sea, the Baltic, and the Gulf of Finland, the pilots wore – both over their flight suits and next to their bodies – a belt and pistol, yellow flying scarf, thick fur-lined flying boots, parachute pack, a life vest, a collapsed one-man life raft, a packet of yellow dye, a flare pistol with multi-colored flares, plus an emergency kit for bailing out.

During winter operations on the Eastern Front, this gear was supplemented by other equipment for emergency landings; this included an insulated flight suit, short skis, ski poles, snow tires, and a compass. All of this was carried in a backpack – along with emergency provisions for eight days – and was stored in the fuselage of the airplane.

While on alert, the pilots made the time pass more quickly with all kinds of activities. Skat, chess, and a card game known as doppelkopf were the favorites. During longer breaks in the action pilots could also be found hunting, playing sports, painting or building models, or planting and cultivating vegetables and flowers. Still others whittled out artistic Geschwader "victory sticks" or decorated their own readiness rooms. Many pilots kept busy as amateur musicians. The accordion, trumpet, and violin were the preferred instruments.

A visitor to the pilots' dispersal areas would also encounter all kinds of animals. There were numerous dogs of varying breeds – dachshunds, mastiffs, schnauzers, terriers, and funny-looking mutts from all the countries the Geschwader had passed through. "Peterle", "Hexe", "Ivan", "Chica", and "Sonja" all lived with and for their pilots. During redeployments most of the dogs flew with their masters in the luggage compartment of the Bf 109 or Fw 190. In doing so, they sometimes inadvertently found themselves in a dogfight! Many a brave Staffelhund was taken as a Russian "prisoner-of-war" when an airfield was vacated in a hurry.

In addition to the dogs, there were other types of animals to be found wandering around the sites. These were generally strictly watched geese, hens, pigs, or cows. All had their pet names, but sooner or later they all ended up in the cooking pot of the Staffel cook.

During a "scramble", pilots were torn from their sleepy relaxation in a lounge chair, from their chess games and intense games of doppelkopf, or from playing with the Staffelhund – suddenly and without warning, yet alert. Minutes later they were racing along at tree-top level or between 4000 – 10000 meters, with the most intense demands placed on their bodies and their senses, sucking oxygen as the altitudes constantly fluctuated, whirling and turning to survive – or perish – in an animal-like, treacherous, merciless struggle. Separated from the warm, green grass, from a freshly dished plate, from a catnap on the lawn, or in wintertime, from the warm command post, to be thrown into the grim battle in the skies.

The seriousness of the war gripped the Geschwader in an incalculable and mysterious way. A pilot took off, fought, and with a single turn became separated from the Staffel, disappearing inside a low cloud bank – never to return from the sortie. Another, caught in the nightmarish fire of a bomber formation, suddenly became transformed with his plane into a ball of flame and in seconds vanished without a trace.

Other Grünherz fighters, suspended from their parachutes, disappeared forever into the waves of the ocean or the endless marshes of the Russian northern front. At dinnertime, their places remained vacant.

Then there were those pilots who, along with their colleagues, landed after the battle as usual. They climbed quietly from their planes, yet something inside them had changed. They had overcome Death and at the same time had participated in it. Now they remained silent, not quite knowing what to say. They stared at the flowers on the taxiway or let their gaze attentively follow a beetle as it scurried along.

Although none of the pilots expressed it vocally, each one knew that he would have to fly until he fell in combat or until the day when peace would come.

Missions and Duties of the Pilots

The missions assigned to the Grünherz fighters were numerous and varied. They were in a constant state of flux throughout the course of the war and were governed by the requirements of the situation both on the ground and in the air.

As their duties, the pilots performed:

Fighter Sweeps

This was the crowning glory of fighter combat. The fighter unit hunted "free", meaning according to its own discretion and the development of combat dynamics, at altitudes which were determined by the flying formations themselves. The intention, of course, was to engage and destroy as many enemy aircraft as possible. During fighter sweep operations, or "freie Jagd", only the combat area – "the hunting preserve" – was specifically established by higher authority.

Escort

Provided for bombers, dive bombers, air transport units, and reconnaissance aircraft. During escort missions, the fighter pilots were tasked with providing defensive cover in the immediate vicinity of their protective charges. A fighter pilot flying escort was not permitted to leave his "flock"; he wasn't permitted to pursue the enemy planes challenging him to battle, nor could he hunt them down and destroy them. He went without personal success.

An explanation is in order with regard to the frequent usage of the terms "Kampf-" and "Jagd-" throughout this book: "Kampfflieger", also known as "Kämpfer" (the German word for "to fight" is "kämpfen") were bomber pilots who dropped bombs from multi-engine aircraft; their role didn't include engaging enemy aircraft in the air!

On the other hand, Jagdflieger, often called simply "Jäger" (jagen = "to hunt"), were those pilots who engaged the enemy in the air.

Ground Attack
using on-board weapons against ground targets in support of friendly ground forces.

Fighter-Bomber Operations
The pilots, whose planes were fitted with a single 250 kg bomb or four 50 kg bombs, flew these types of missions against ground targets such as bridges, storage facilities, train stations, tanks, airfields, artillery and anti-aircraft batteries, as well as shipping. They were called Jagdbomber, or simply "Jabos."

Reconnaissance Operations
For providing visual aerial reconnaissance in areas which were heavily protected by enemy fighters.

Weather Reconnaissance
For determining the weather conditions (cloud base and visibility) over a particular combat sector.

Airfield Protection
Depending on the situation in the air, either two or four pilots found themselves strapped into their planes in preparation for an immediate scramble within a few seconds.

In addition, the 20 mm Flakzüge (anti-aircraft platoons) from the individual Jagdgruppen also provided airfield protection around the clock.

Night Fighter Operations
Night fighter operations using the Bf 109 were only flown temporarily by the pilots of the Geschwader during the short nights over the Volkhov pocket in the northern sector of the Eastern Front (summer 1942).

There was no type of fighter operation with which the Geschwader was not familiar. With regards to these mixed and often changing roles, a popular advertising slogan was borrowed and applied: "The Geschwader glues – pastes – and patches everything!"

The number of aircraft used in these operations varied depending on the situation in the air. The smallest and most flexible unit in fighter combat was the Rotte consisting of two aircraft, led by the Rottenführer (or "element leader") and accompanied at his side by the Rottenflieger ("wingman"), also called the "Katschmarek." When the Rottenführer executed an attack he was protected at his back by his "Katschmarek." Two Rotten flying parallel made up a Schwarm, led by a Schwarmführer. Multiple Schwärme (usually two to three) formed a Staffel, while multiple Staffeln (usually three) comprised a Jagdgruppe and multiple Jagdgruppen (usually three Gruppen) made up the Geschwader.

At the start of the Battle of Britain the Geschwader flew in Geschwader strength of 60 to 80 Bf 109s under the guidance of the Kommodore. On the Eastern Front the operational strength was reduced for tactical reasons, usually down to the level of the Rotte and Schwarm. Only later, during the defense of the Reich, operations were once again conducted in larger formations (at the Staffel or Gruppe level).

The "Black Men"

The outstanding successes achieved by the pilots of the Grünherzgeschwader wouldn't have been possible without the dedicated work of the industrious men of the support personnel, whether in the headquarters, Staffeln, headquarters companies or signals units. Because of their black work overalls, the ground personnel were simply called "black men."

Their activities and functions were multifarious. Within the realm of flight activity, the "black men" were employed as aircraft mechanics, aircraft maintenance crewmen, engine mechanics, electricians, painters, leather workers, carpenters, parachute and safety technicians, radio maintenance technicians, equipment administrators, radio and telegraph operators, armorers, refuellers, vehicle drivers, inspectors, and anti-aircraft soldiers, among other duties. General troop personnel were utilized as headquarters and command post clerks, technical clerks, accounting clerks, cooks, medics, and clothing and supply administrators.

As with the pilots, the technical personnel came from all parts of the country: From Graz to Flensburg and from Aachen to Königsberg. The location where the individual Gruppen were first established played a certain role in determining where the ground personnel had their roots.

With the outbreak of war the bulk of active soldiers was beefed up by numerous reservists, who for the most part were called up out of technical civilian occupations. The ages varied between 18 and 50 years.

Along with the general support personnel in the Staffel, there were also technical personnel whose job it was to keep the fighter aircraft of the Staffel operationally ready. The maintenance crews in the Staffel were subordinate to an Oberwerkmeister. Each airplane was maintained by a crew chief and an assistant crew chief.

A Waffenoberfeldwebel was, along with his armorers (also called "Waffenjodler" – lit. "weapons yodlers"), responsible for the weapons of the aircraft. Just as the Funkfeldwebel with his radio technicians was responsible for the proper functioning of the aircraft's radio equipment.

Major work such as shell damage, engine change, plus all repairs to vehicles, radio and other equipment was carried out by the technical personnel of the well-equipped maintenance platoon (Werftzug) of the HQ company.

The "black men", whether technician, driver, armorer, or radioman, were certainly not the most smartly-dressed soldiers in appearance, but they worked genuine miracles in a "Luftwaffe day" – those days of 24 hours work time.

After the maintenance work had been done, when aircraft and weapons stood ready for combat, they sank exhausted into their bunks. Like their pilots, with whom they had a brotherly and faithful bond, and with whom they shared tips for ensuring smooth aircraft handling, they also possessed a unique talent for falling into a deep sleep. The world could have collapsed around them without them waking up, but the slightest whistle or call by the Oberwerkmeister magically summoned them from their dream sleep back to their planes. Even today, it's amazing how they managed to turn over a frozen engine in the merciless cold of a Russian winter, how they coaxed out that first unwilling iron cough within the briefest span of time – a cough which eventually turned into a hesitant, reluctant growl and finally became the deep-sounding roar of a high-performance machine. At the same time, they were just as ready to jump from their sleeping bunks to prove themselves in combat as infantrymen.

The "black men" could always be counted on!

Aircraft and Vehicles of the Geschwader

During the war's first years, the Grünherzgeschwader was equipped with various models of the Messerschmitt Bf 109 single-seat fighter. As the war progressed the Geschwader's Gruppen converted to nearly every variant of the single-seat Focke-Wulf Fw 190 fighter.

The total overall strength of operational aircraft in the Geschwader fluctuated according to the number of the subordinate Staffeln and Gruppen. It varied between 120 and 160 fighters, a figure which, in practice, was reduced considerably following air combat or ground fire.

The Bf 109F was an elegant, light, low-wing monoplane of all-metal construction. The aircraft was powered by a 12-cylinder Daimler-Benz DB 601 inline engine developing approximately 1400 hp. Additional characteristics of the Bf 109F: three-blade metal propeller, 400 liter fuel tank, maximum endurance of 1.2 hrs. The pilot sat in a small enclosed cockpit from which he fired the aircraft's fixed, forward-firing guns; in short, he used the entire aircraft as a gunsight.

After a flight time of approximately 70 minutes, the notorious red caution light came on in front of the pilot's seat, signaling to the pilot that he had only a few minutes left before landing became necessary. Landing gear and tailwheel were retractable. Takeoff roll was 300 meters; landing required 600 meters. Horizontal speed near the ground was 540 kilometers per hour (kmh); maximum speed at 6000 meters altitude was 650 kmh. Service ceiling was 11800 m. Landing speed was 150 kmh. Range was 525 kilometers with a takeoff weight of approx. 3000 kg.

The standard armament of the Bf 109F consisted of two MG 17 7.9 mm guns installed above the engine and firing through the propeller arc, plus an MG 151 of either 15 or 20 mm firing through the engine block. Two additional MG 151s could be installed as field conversion kits in the form of underwing gondola packs.

With the Bf 109G variant flown later in the war, an increase in firepower to two MG 131s and an MG 151 caused another change which yet again altered the "face" of the Bf 109. Because of the characteristic bumps on either side of the engine housing, caused by the MG 131 guns, the troops gave the aircraft the nickname of "Beule" (bump or knot)

After the Bf 109, the Fw 190A-5 was for a long time the standard aircraft of the Geschwader. The all-metal low-wing monoplane was fitted with various field conversion kits, depending on the missions within the Gruppen. The compact, robust fighter was powered by a BMW 801 radial engine developing 1700 hp. Additional technical data: three-blade metal propeller; fuel capacity was 400 liters with a maximum endurance of 1.3 hrs;

range was 650 kilometers at minimum fuel consumption; maximum speed at 6900 m was 660 kmh; service ceiling was 11500 m; takeoff weight was approximately 4000 kg; takeoff roll was 370 m and landing roll was 500 m at a speed of 180 kmh.

The armament of the Fw 190 varied depending on the model. Standard armament, however, included two MG 131 13 mm machine guns above the engine and two MG 151/20s in the right and left wing roots. These weapons were all synchronized to fire through the propeller arc. Up to six MG 151s could be carried on the outer wings.

The armament installed in the airplanes were sighted by the armorers to about 400 meters distance when the aircraft was flying horizontal.

Both in the Bf 109 and the Fw 190 the pilot sighted through a reflexive gunsight (in German "Reflexvisier", or "Revi"). The "Revi" was illuminated and was mounted immediately above the instrument panel inside the aircraft's cockpit.

The fighters were equipped with HF (later also VHF) air-to-air and air-to-ground radios, so that the pilots were in constant contact not only with each other, but also with the ground control sites as well.

The Bf 109 and Fw 190 fighters could rapidly be converted to and used as fighter-bombers for striking ground and naval targets.

Both fighter types were sometimes equipped with expendable drop tanks for increasing flying time/range. The Bf 109 had a single 300 liter auxiliary fuel tank underneath the fuselage, while the Fw 190 carried two, one under each wing. The range could then be extended to over 1000 km.

In addition to the fighter aircraft used in operations, the Jagdgruppen also had various types of liaison and courier aircraft, including:

Heinkel Blitz (He 70)
Junkers (W 34)
Focke-Wulf "Weihe" (Fw 58)
(also known as "Leukoplast-Bomber" - "band-aid bomber" in pilot's jargon)
Klemm (KL 35)
Fieseler "Storch" (Fi 156)

These aircraft were used for limited air transport of personnel, equipment, and mail.

Rescue operations for shot-down and crash-landed pilots were conducted using the Fieseler "Storch", which could be fitted with ski runners for winter operations. Since there were virtually no helicopters operating during the Second World War, the "Storch" was the preferred airplane for short takeoffs and landings in difficult terrain.

The Grünherzgeschwader and its three Jagdgruppen were fully motorized, possessing around 160 vehicles. When transferring from one airfield to another the pilots initially flew their own airplanes. An advance detachment, comprised primarily of leading technical personnel, followed along in one or more transport aircraft. These transports – mostly Junkers Ju 52s – were temporarily provided to the Geschwader for the move by a higher command official. With the arrival of the technical advance team at the new base and the examination of the fighters having been completed, the Staffel or Gruppe was once again more or less operational.

The main column, with the bulk of the Geschwader, carried personnel and equipment via land routes, in rare instances by rail.

A single Jagdgruppe with its headquarters company and three Staffeln had, as its own vehicles, on average:

5 motorcycles (some with sidecar)
11 cars
25 trucks with trailers
12 trucks and specialized vehicles
(such as: tank trucks, cranes, starters, fire trucks, ambulances, communications vans)
53 vehicles total

In addition to this motor pool, numerous captured enemy vehicles also were utilized during the course of the war.

The Long Journey of the Grünherzgeschwader

During the five years of its existence, the Grünherzgeschwader traversed a long and difficult course.

Innumerable deployments in the air and on the ground carried the Geschwader's units to over 200 airfields as its units bounded from flashpoint to flashpoint.

The pilots of the Grünherzgeschwader flew and fought over Poland, France, Belgium, Holland, England, over Yugoslavia, Russia, Finland, Rumania, and finally over Germany itself in the defense of the Reich.

The men of the ground support crews followed their pilots in vehicles carrying all the technical equipment. During these long overland transport journeys, the drivers in the Geschwader demonstrated their worth time and time again. They maneuvered their vehicles under the most difficult road and weather conditions, travelling thousands of kilometers and . . . they always reached their destination!

Establishment

The history of Jagdgeschwader 54 began originally with the establishment of the three base Gruppen. Prior to being subordinated to the Geschwaderstab in July of 1940, these Jagdgruppen were initially established and operated under different designations. They were organized at different times and at different airbases.

I/JG 54 was formed from I /JG 70 and was christened on 15 September 1939 in Herzogenaurach near Nuremberg. The ground crewmen were therefore recruited primarily from the Franconian region. As its coat-of-arms, the Gruppe carried the symbol of the city of Nuremberg.

II/JG 54 was the oldest Gruppe in the Geschwader. It was formed from the former Austrian Jagdgruppe "Wien-Aspern" which had been established back in 1938. After Austria was annexed, the Gruppe was taken into the Luftwaffe with the interim designation of I/JG 76, then eventually renamed II/JG 54.

The members of this Gruppe were primarily Austrians. The Gruppe carried the "Lion of Aspern" in its coat-of-arms.

III/JG 54 was established on 15 July 1939 in Jesau and Gutenfeld in East Prussia. It was primarily made up of East Prussian personnel. Until being resubordinated to JG 54 the unit carried the designation I/JG 21. The Gruppe carried the coat-of-arms of the Knights of the Order as its symbol.

The Polish Campaign

Only II/JG 54 (formerly I/JG 76) and III/JG 54 (formerly I/JG 21) took part in the Polish campaign from 1 September to 6 October 1939. The pilots flew their first front-line operations of the Second World War in Bf 109Ds from airfields in East Prussia, Silesia, and Czechoslovakia. These missions included escort for bombers and Stukas, fighter sweeps and ground attack. During the course of the campaign both Jagdgruppen occupied airfields in Poland, including Bialystok and Camicy near Radom.

The first victories were scored during the Polish campaign, during which the first decorations were also awarded.

While the Polish operations were ongoing I/JG 54 remained in readiness at the Herzogenaurach airfield.

"Sitzkrieg" in the West

From 9 October 1939 until 10 May 1940 all three of the Geschwader's Gruppen operated in the air defense role and were stationed at airfields in western and southern Germany.

I/JG 54 was based at airfields in Böblingen, Friedrichshafen and Eutingen bei Horb.

II/JG 54 was in Gelnhausen, Rhein-Main, Walldorf, and Ober-Olm.

III/JG 54 operated from Plantlünne, Hopsten, Krefeld, Münster, and Mönchengladbach.

Working from these airfields, small formations carried out fighter sweep operations for protecting the airspace up to the French border. Repeated contact with the enemy was made during these missions, during which combat ensued with lone French and British reconnaissance aircraft (Moranes, Spitfires, and Blenheims).

It was during this time period that the Gruppen began converting from the Bf 109D to the Bf 109E.

The Campaign Against France

The three Gruppen of the Geschwader took part in the French campaign under frequently changing tasking assignments. During the campaign the pilots flew ahead of the advancing German army units, providing escort for bombers and Stukas as well as conducting low-level strikes and fighter sweeps which ranged deep into the enemy's rear areas. The pilots were in combat with French fighters and bombers such as: Morane 406, Bloch 131, Dewoitine 520, Breguet 693, Potez 631, and MS 406.

The first operations of the French campaign were launched while the pilots were still based at German airfields; later they flew from Dutch, Belgian, and French bases, to include Ghent, Evreux, Vitry en Artois, Poix, Paris-Orly, and Orleans.

Among the more significant roles in France were escort of German bomber formations and fighter sweeps during the concentrated attack by the Luftwaffe on 3 June 1940 against airfields and aviation industrial sites around Paris, known as "Operation Paula."

Just as important was the protection given to German bomber and Stuka units during strikes against the retreating British Expeditionary Forces in the Dunkirk pocket at the end of May/beginning of June 1940.

It was during these missions that the units first became involved in heavy dogfighting with British Spitfires and Hurricanes operating from bases in the south of England.

Air Defense in Holland

With the capitulation of the French, on 21 June 1940 the three Jagdgruppen of the Geschwader were moved back to Holland to carry out air defense operations and get some rest and recuperation (R & R).

In this phase of restocking men and aircraft, from June 1940 until the beginning of August 1940, the units were based as follows:

I/JG 54 in Eindhoven and Schipol
II/JG 54 in Waalhaven and Vlissingen
III/JG 54 in Soesterberg and Bergen am See

During operations in Holland the pilots of the Geschwader intercepted and shot down lone British recce and bomber aircraft, mostly Bristol Blenheims.

III Gruppe suffered heavy personnel and material losses during a night raid by British bombers on 23-24 July 1940 against the Soesterberg airbase.

The Battle of Britain

At the end of July/beginning of August 1940 the Luftwaffe High Command pooled together ten fighter and three attack Geschwader on the Channel front. With a view toward the planned invasion of the British Isles by German ground troops, the Luftwaffe – with its Kampfflieger, Stuka, and Jagdgeschwadern – was to gain air supremacy over the Royal Air Force and thereby pave the way for a large-scale landing by ground forces in England.

On 6 August 1940 Jagdgeschwader 54 and its three subordinate Jagdgruppen moved to the well-concealed airfields in the area of Calais:

Geschwaderstab and I/JG 54 in Campagne
II/JG 54 in Harlinghem, later in Campagne
III/JG 54 in Guines

For the first time in the Geschwader's history the Staffeln and Gruppen lay in close proximity to each other – in "touching distance" – so to speak. It was during the tough fighting on the Channel that a particularly close camaraderie developed, not only between the pilots and "black men" of the ground support, but also between officers, NCOs, and the enlisted ranks. During the Battle of Britain, the Geschwader began to grow into a large, solid family of flyers.

The pilots were generally employed in Geschwader formations of 60 to 80 aircraft. Three to four operations per day wasn't a rare occurrence. With shell damage suffered during brutal dogfights with British Spitfires and Hurricanes, the number of operational aircraft rapidly dwindled during the course of the day. The "black men" were always found sweating away between missions and during the night, repairing the planes and getting them operational again as quickly as possible.

There were sometimes vicious tight-turning battles, during which neither side was able to fire a shot because no one was able to get his guns to bear on another.

The aerial combat carried out against British fighters brought our pilots many victories, but at the same time it also cost them bitter sacrifices and severe injuries.

The missions of Jagdgeschwader 54 during the air offensive against England were numerous and varied:

- Fighter sweeps over southern England as far as London
- Escort for friendly Kampf- and Stukageschwader units during their attacks on convoys and other shipping in the Channel and Thames estuary, as well as on airfields in the greater London area and military targets along the coast, such as Manston, Dover, Lympne, Ramsgate and Hawkinge
- Fighter protection for air-sea rescue operations, meaning for those air-sea rescue planes and rescue launches recovering pilots who had been shot down in the Channel
- Providing fighter protection against further attacks over the Channel for German bombers and Stukas, many of them shot up, returning from raids on England
- Air defense over the Franco-Belgian coast, providing a barrier against potential British reconnaissance and bomber aircraft flying daytime missions into our jump-off area.
- Fighter-bomber missions for striking military targets along the east coast of England and shipping targets in the Thames estuary and Channel, as well as carrying out nuisance raids on London

These operations, flown at altitudes between 4,000 and 10,000 meters, were directed by Jagdfliegerführer 2, the Jafü, from its command center in Wissant (later Le Touquet), while specific tasking was made from within the Geschwader.

During this phase of combat the Geschwader's pilots were faced with demanding responsibilities. Aside from those exceptions dictated by the weather, they were kept in constant readiness with full flight gear from the crack of dawn until the last glimmer of sunset. Stand-down days occurred only seldom, and these were utilized for sightseeing in the little town of Lille "the proper way."

Our pilots encountered several obstacles during the Battle of Britain. Foremost among these was the unfamiliar flight operations over the Channel and the long approach to London, during which the British fighters had the advantage of fighting over their own territory. Even when they had to make emergency landings after being shot up, the British were still "in their own backyard."

For operations against London, the limited 1.2 hrs of flight time for the Bf 109 was a certain handicap. On escort missions, fuel was barely sufficient for a round trip flight. When enemy contact was made the engine was pushed to its maximum performance, and the fuel tanks were then very quickly flown to "empty." Without exception, this precipitated either a ditching in the Channel on the return flight, or, if the pilot was lucky, a belly-landing on the French coast.

If a pilot parachuted down into the waves of the Channel, he got free of his parachute, automatically inflated his life vest and attempted to clamber into his small one-man life-boat, which could be inflated by means of a bellows. A yellow packet of dye, thrown into the water by the pilot, marked the "landing site" of the unfortunate flyer and enabled him to be spotted and rescued more easily.

The procedure was similar when ditching an airplane. Normally, the Bf 109 sank within two to five minutes, during which time the pilot had to free himself from the aircraft and set himself afloat.

If everything went smoothly, a pilot falling into the "drink" was fished out either by an He 59 air-sea rescue plane or one of the Heer's modified engineer assault boats. These boats were stationed at several points along the coast from Dunkirk to Boulogne.

The Luftwaffe's leadership ordered a "rejuvenation cure" for the Kommodore of those Jagdgeschwader operating against England; accordingly, Hannes Trautloft assumed command of Jagdgeschwader 54 on 25 August 1940, replacing Major Mettig.

The command personnel of the Geschwader during the Battle of Britain was:

Kommodore JG 54:	Major Trautloft
Kommandeur I/JG 54:	Hauptmann von Bonin
Kommandeur II/JG 54:	Hauptmann Hrabak
Kommandeur III/JG 54:	Hauptmann Ultsch
	Oberleutnant Scholz (temporary)
	Hauptmann Lignitz

Staffelkapitäne:	
1 Staffel:	Oberleutnant Seiler
	Oberleutnant Rumpf (temporary)
	Oberleutnant Köderitzch
2 Staffel:	Oberleutnant Unger
3 Staffel:	Oberleutnant Schmoller-Haldy
4 Staffel:	Oberleutnant Philipp
5 Staffel:	Oberleutnant von Aspern
	Oberleutnant Mütherich
6 Staffel:	Oberleutnant Stangel
	Oberleutnant Eckerle
7 Staffel:	Oberleutnant Scholz
8 Staffel:	Oberleutnant Egger
	Oberleutnant Hausmann
9 Staffel:	Oberleutnant Schneider
	Oberleutnant Hausmann (temporary)
	Oberleutnant Bob

It was at the Channel that the first pilots of the Grünherzgeschwader were awarded the Knight's Cross to the Iron Cross upon scoring 20 victories: Hauptmann Dieter Hrabak, Kommandeur of II/JG 54 on 24 October 1940, Oberleutnant Hans Philipp, Staffelkapitän of 4 Staffel on 4 November 1940, and Hauptmann Arnold Lignitz, Kommandeur of III/JG 54 on 8 November 1940.

During the Battle of Britain, the British fighter pilots took off to do battle with the Germans from many airfields, primarily those at Biggin Hill, Northolt, Kenley, Hornchurch, Southend, and Eastchurch. The names of these airfields remain etched forever in the memories of the Grünherz pilots, along with the "endearing" appellation given to German aircraft over the British radio – "bandits." The "bandits" labeled their English "colleagues" in radio communications with the somewhat friendlier title of "Indianer" (Indians).

When German Kampfgeschwader units and their escorting fighters were forming up at a particular assembly point, there were often concentrations of 500 to 600 friendly aircraft within a very small airspace. Despite this, there were just as few air collisions as in the turbulent aerial combat with British fighters over the British Isles. The Geschwader lost eight Bf 109s in such collisions on both sides of the Channel, while virtually all the pilots involved were able to bale out of their stricken planes.

During the Battle of Britain, from 12 August to 1 December 1940, Jagdgeschwader 54 lost a total of 43 pilots – nearly 40 percent of the total number of flying personnel on strength. Of these, 20 were officers and 23 NCOs. 18 pilots were killed, including the Kommandeur of III Gruppe, Hauptmann Ultsch, and the Staffelkapitän of 5 Staffel, Oberleutnant von Aspern. The Staffelkapitän of 1 Staffel, Oberleutnant Seiler, was shot down in flames over the Channel on one of the first missions in a dogfight with Spitfires; he was forced to take to his chute and was fished from the water a few hours later by the German Marine. He rejoined the Geschwader in the spring of 1941. Two pilots were involved in fatal accidents, thirteen were missing in action, and ten were known to have been taken as British POWs.

The 43 losses stand in comparison to 238 victories scored. On one of the last operations on the Channel front 3 Staffel was bounced by Spitfires and lost Oberfeldwebel Knippscher, who fortunately was able to bale out. The Staffel had begun operations against England with twelve pilots. After the loss of Knippscher 3 Staffel had just two pilots left, namely Oberleutnant Kinzinger and the Staffelkapitän, Oberleutnant Schmoller-Haldy. A transfer to the rear for the bloodied Staffeln and Gruppen for rest and recuperation purposes became more and more pressing.

Rejuvenation at German Airbases

Storm, rains, fog and muddy airfields in the late fall of 1940 prevented further large-scale operations against England. Only "garbage missions" continued. The air offensive was broken off in the late fall/winter of 1940 once the High Command realized that the establishment of air superiority over England had failed, the prerequisite for the ground invasion codenamed Operation "Seelöwe." By Gruppen, the Jagdgeschwader involved were pulled back to airfields in the rear area for recuperation.

Completely exhausted, I/JG 54 was transferred to Jever as early as 27 September 1940 where it was subordinated to Jagdgeschwader 1 until May of 1941, providing protection for the German Bight. From Jever, the Gruppe provided short-term detachments to the airfields at Wesermünde, Westerland, and Groningen in Holland.

II/JG 54 took up its winter R & R quarters at the airbase in Delmenhorst from 3 December 1940 to 23 January 1941.

III/JG 54 was transferred from Guines on 21 October 1940 to once again provide airspace protection for Holland, taking up residence at the airfields of Schipol, Katwijk, Hamstede, and De Kooey. On 4 December 1940 the Gruppe also went on R & R, transferring to the Dortmund airbase until 15 January 1941.

The winter time of peace was used by the units to bring personnel, aircraft and equipment back up to strength for future operations. Each member of the Geschwader was able to take some time off to go on well-deserved leave. The pilots of the Geschwader spent a combined ski holiday in Kitzbühel, during which time not only was it possible to reestablish human contact but there were also several broken bones logged.

Air Defense in the Area of Le Mans – Cherbourg

The phase of winter rest in Dortmund and Delmenhorst was quickly broken on 15 January 1941 by transfer orders to Le Mans (200 kilometers southwest of Paris).

Geschwaderstab, II/JG 54 and III/JG 54 assumed protection over Normandy for two months, operating from the airfields at Le Mans and the forward airstrip at Cherbourg. I/JG 54 remained in Jever during this time. The air situation over Le Mans was relatively quiet, so that the Staffeln and Gruppen could – for a while – provide increased ground and air training. Athletics and shooting with all types of firearms, an NCO training detachment, plus weapons familiarization played an important role during this time.

The "knighting of the fighter pilots", which every newly assigned pilot was given by the Kommodore at the first-ever Geschwader pilots' night, was an unforgettable event for all those taking part. The "Le Mans Interlude" came to an end in late March of 1941.

Operations in the Balkans

On 29 March 1941 Jagdgeschwader 54, together with its Stab, II/JG 54 and III/JG 54, was unexpectedly air and ground transported from Le Mans to Austria in order to take part in the campaign against Yugoslavia.

The pilots of the Geschwader flew along the snow-covered Alpine ranges, making an interim landing in Salzburg before continuing on to their assigned bases:

Geschwaderstab and II/JG 54 in Graz
III/JG 54 in Parendorf, later Arad (Rumania)

I/JG 54 continued to stay behind in Jever during the Balkans campaign, still subordinated to Jagdgeschwader 1. The ground columns completed the 1630 kilometer journey from Le Mans to Graz without any serious incidents. A daily journey of over 400 km was not uncommon, and the drivers performed outstandingly.

On 6 April 1941 the Geschwader units of the Luftwaffe, including Jagdgeschwader 54, overflew the Yugoslavian border. Airfields and military sites in the Belgrade area were the targets of the first attacks.

As the campaign progressed the Geschwader's Staffeln, armed with the Bf 109E, conducted fighter sweeps and ground strikes, primarily targeting locomotives, with the goal of disrupting all enemy movements.

Among the enemy aircraft encountered were Bf 109Ds, bought from Germany by the Yugoslavs at an earlier date.

During the campaign, units of the Geschwader occupied airfields in Rumania, Hungary and Yugoslavia, including Arad, Deta, Fünfkirchen, Bijeljina, Panchevo, and Semlin-Belgrade.

When four Ju 52 transports landed at the forward air support site of Bijeljina (approximately 100 km east of Belgrade) the "black men" were called upon to prove themselves in ground combat for the first time. The airfield was attacked by numerically superior, generally irregular enemy forces. Both sides suffered fallen and wounded casualties. During a tough defensive fight, in which the Geschwader's pilots supported the action with ground attacks, Bijeljina was finally taken.

Once the last remnants of the Yugoslav army were encircled in Bosnia, they capitulated on 17 April 1941. The Grünherz fighters had scored 376 kills up to this point since the beginning of the war.

Jagdgeschwader 54 assembled itself with all its units at the large civil airport of Semlin near Belgrade. Since all the bridges over the Danube had been blown up, the difficult task of transporting the ground columns was undertaken using Danube barges, which had been provisionally lashed together to form ferries.

In Semlin the Grünherz pilots were given orders to hand over all their Bf 109E fighters to Jagdgeschwader 77. In exchange, the Geschwader was to be re-equipped with the Bf 109F at the Stolp-Reitz airfield in Pomerania.

Beginning on the 3rd of May 1941, ground units of the Geschwaderstab, II and III Gruppe set out from Belgrade to Pomerania using rail transport or under their own power, covering a distance of some 2000 kilometers.

The Balkan campaign demonstrated yet again that the Geschwader, both in spirit and in weapons operations, was on the right path for continued cooperative growth.

The bulk of the Geschwader began arriving in Stolp-Reitz on 12 May 1941.

"Red Star" vs. "Green Heart" – The Grünherzgeschwader in the East

1941

After the entire Geschwader had converted over to the Bf 109F, and following intense flight, military, technical and tactical training by all its soldiers, the Geschwader – including the recently rejoined I Gruppe – transferred to prepared airfields in East Prussia.

This action brought the Geschwader operationally under the I Fliegerkorps commanded by General der Flieger Förster, within Generaloberst Keller's Luftflotte 1 district.

The Geschwader was temporarily reinforced by II/JG 53 under Hauptmann Bretnütz.

On 21 June 1941, the day prior to Operation "Barbarossa", the units of the Geschwader were to be found in readiness at the following airbases:

Trakehnen: Geschwaderstab JG 54
Lindental: I/JG 54
Trakehnen: II/JG 54
Blumenfeld: III/JG 54
Gerlinden: II/JG 53

Luftflotte 1 was given the task of using its Kampf- and Sturzkampfgeschwader units, along with Aufklärerstaffeln and Jagdgeschwader 54 to support Heeresgruppe Nord (with 16 and 18 Armee, plus Panzergruppe 4) from East Prussia as it advanced in a drive toward Leningrad.

During the first days of fighting the pilots of the Grünherzgeschwader mainly flew escort missions for Kampfgeschwader KG 1, KG 76 and KG 77 during their attacks on Russian airfields. As the advance progressed eastward, they were given the responsibility of clearing enemy planes from the skies over Heeresgruppe Nord.

On 22 June 1941 at 0305 hrs, the Grünherzgeschwader overflew the front lines with 120 aircraft as escort for the Kampfgeschwader units striking the airfields at Kovno, Kedainiai and Ponyevesh.

The Russian campaign had begun, and with it a long and fateful journey for the Grünherzgeschwader. The slow and tiresome advance of the Geschwader's ground personnel was made along dusty, congested and miserable roads through Lithuania, Estonia, Latvia, and via Dünaburg (Daugavpils), Pleskau, Ostrow, and Luga.

In comparison, the pilots transferred from one airfield to another quite rapidly with a small number of key technical personnel transported by air.

During the advance on Leningrad they were constantly embroiled in numerous air battles. Of particular significance were the battles over Dünaburg on 30 June 1941 with 65 victories and the fighting over the Ostrow bridgehead from 4 to 7 July 1941 which brought 109 kills. As early as 1 August 1941 Leutnant Ostermann scored the 1000th victory for the Grünherzgeschwader. The 16th Armee reached Lake Ilmen on 31 July 1941 and the 18th Armee the Gulf of Finland on 17 August 1941. By mid September troops of Heeresgruppe Nord stood at the defensive perimeter of Leningrad. Here, however, the operation finally ground to a halt.

Jagdgeschwader 54 occupied the airbase at Siverskaya on 5 September 1941 and Krasnogvardeysk (also known as Gatschina) a few days later. Along with Staraya Russa and Rjelbitzi (in pilot's jargon "Ringelpietz"), these two airfields were to be the main base of operations for the Grünherzgeschwader in the northern sector of the Eastern Front.

From the middle of September 1941 the Geschwader's pilots flew in several operations per day as escort for bomber and Stuka formations supporting the Heer and during their attacks on the Soviet Baltic Fleet in the Kronstadt harbor from 21 to 25 September.

Fighter sweeps in Rotte and Schwarm strength both over the front and deep in the enemy hinterlands brought additional victories for the Grünherz flyers. Many locomotives were destroyed in strafing attacks, seriously crippling the Soviets' supply lines. At that time, the areas of combat operations were the "iron-bearing" regions around the Gulf of Finland – Leningrad, Neva, Lake Ladoga, Volkhov, Lake Ilmen, Dem'yansk.

The Grünherz pilots were kept abreast of any Russian aircraft overflying the front by observation posts such as "Bruno", "Hildegard" and "Leopold" stationed along the entire front. The pilots were immediately warned via radio, enabling targets to be quickly engaged.

The frontal sector protected by the Grünherzgeschwader ranged from the Gulf of Finland to Dem'yansk and covered approximately 400 kilometers.

On 24 August 1941 the commander of 4 Staffel, Oberleutnant "Fips" Philipp, was the first pilot of the Geschwader to be awarded the Oak Leaves to the Knight's Cross for 62 kills. On 30 September 1941 the Kommandeur of III Gruppe, Hauptmann Lignitz, was shot down. He was able to take to his parachute, but fell into the center of Leningrad and has been missing in action since that time. The new commander of III Gruppe on 1 October 1941 was Hauptmann "Seppl" Seiler, whose 1 Staffel was taken over by Oberleutnant Heinz Lange.

By the 8th of November 1941 the Geschwader had seen 34 of its members fall in combat on the Eastern Front, 27 pilots and 7 ground personnel. Ten soldiers were missing in action. One of the successful pilots of the Geschwader, Oberleutnant Ruland of 3 Staffel, was fatally injured in a bombing raid during the night of 1-2 August. Just a few nights before the same Staffel had already lost their trusted "Spiess", Oberfeldwebel (later Oberleutnant) Braden, who was seriously injured in another night bombing attack.

On 20 December 1941 the former commander of I Gruppe, Hauptmann von Selle, was transferred. His successor was Hauptmann Eckerle, whose 6 Staffel was to be commanded by Oberleutnant Sattig.

1942

The year 1942 was "rung in" by a heavy bombing raid from the Soviets on 2 January 1942 on the Siverskaya airbase. Personnel injury was light, but ten aircraft were destroyed. The thermometer showed 45 degrees Celsius below!

On 14 February 1942 the Kommandeur of I Gruppe, Hauptmann Eckerle, fell in combat. His replacement was Hauptmann "Fips" Philipp, whose 4 Staffel command was assumed by Oberleutnant Wengel.

A few days later, on 23 February, the Staffelkapitän of 3 Staffel was critically injured; Hauptmann Schmoller-Haldy had led the Staffel from the first day of the war. He was succeeded by Hauptmann Koall.

On 12 March 1942 Hauptmann Philipp was the first pilot in the Geschwader to receive the Swords to the Knight's Cross of the Iron Cross. On 31 March 1942 "Fips" scored his 100th kill.

The Geschwader was able to report its 2000th victory on 4 April, made by Oberfeldwebel Klemm.

Among the most outstanding missions flown by the Geschwader in 1942 are:

- escort for German bomber and Stuka unit during repeated strikes against Russian warships in Leningrad harbor in April 1942
- fighter protection for transport aircraft during the resupply of the Kholm fortress (beginning 21 January 1942) and the besieged II Armeekorps in the Dem'yansk pocket (9 February 1942 to 31 October 1942)
- fighter protection for army units during the Battle of Volkhov (13 January 1942 to 27

July 1942). It was over the Volkhov salient that the pilots of the Geschwader flew the first night operations with the Bf 109 in the East. 56 kills were scored without a loss to themselves. Leutnant Leykauf demonstrated particular aptitude as a "night fighter."
- fighter protection for bomber and Stuka formations attacking Soviet supply routes over Lake Ladoga.
- strafing attacks with fighter bombers against supply ships on Lake Ladoga.
- fighter protection for the anti-aircraft armed "Siebel ferries", which unsuccessfully operated from the Finnish port of Lathenpohja on Lake Ladoga in the summer of 1942 in an attempt to sink Russian supply vessels on Lake Ladoga.
As fighter protection for the "Siebel ferries" 1 Staffel under Oberleutnant Lange and 2 Staffel under Oberleutnant Graf von Matuschka were transferred to the Finnish airbase at Petäjärvi near Viipuri. 7 Staffel under Oberleutnant "Hein" Wübke was also temporarily pulled up to Finland in the summer of 1942 to engage Russian supply ships on Lake Ladoga.
- participation in the large-scale defensive battle at Rzhev in the central sector of the Eastern Front in August of 1942.
- fighter protection of the Luftwaffe's bomber units and for the Heer during the Battle of Velikiye Luki and the Valdai Heights (from 1 December 1942).

The number of pilots in the Geschwader totaled 140 on 26 May 1942, of which 47 were officers, 78 NCOs and 15 were enlisted ranks.

As the second officer in the Geschwader to be so recognized, Oberleutnant Ostermann (Staffelkapitän of 7 Staffel) was presented with the Swords to the Knight's Cross on 17 May 1942 after 100 victories. He was shot down and killed by Russian fighters on 9 August 1942 during one of his long range fighter sweeps behind the Lake Ilmen front. His successor as Staffelkapitän of 7 Staffel was Oberleutnant Fink.

6 Staffel's commander, Hauptmann Sattig, was declared missing in action from 10 August 1942 following a dogfight over Rzhev. His replacement as Kapitän of 6 Staffel was to be Leutnant Beisswenger.

On 14 September 1942 the Grünherzgeschwader reports its 3000th aerial victory, achieved by Leutnant Heyer.

Hauptmann "Gnom" Wandel, commander of 5 Staffel, fell on 7 October 1942 after 75 victories while in combat with Russian fighters southeast of Lake Ilmen. His Staffel was taken over by Leutnant Horst Hannig as a temporary commander; beginning on 11 November 1942 Oberleutnant Steindl became the Staffelkapitän.

Oberleutnant Heinz Lange, Staffelkapitän of 1 Staffel, initially took over as Staffelkapitän of 3/JG 51 on 25 October 1942 and then became Kommandeur of IV/JG 51 Mölders. His replacement was the young Leutnant Nowotny.

The Geschwader lost a courageous pilot on 6 October 1942 when Unteroffizier Pfeifer died in combat. He had been the 1941 world downhill skiing champion.

On 27 October 1942 the trusted Kommandeur of II Gruppe, Major Dieter Hrabak, was transferred as Kommodore of Jagdgeschwader 52. The new commander of JG 54 as of 19 November 1942 was Hauptmann "Assi" Hahn.

1943

During the winter months of 1942-1943 the Grünherz fighters stalked their quarry over the key regions uninterrupted until the last rays of sunshine – in the frost, snowstorms and low clouds of those gray days. With their incessant labors and under the most trying of conditions, the "black men" ensured the pilots were always ready to take off.

The 19th of February 1943 was a particularly significant day. Feldwebel Kittel scored the 4000th victory of the Geschwader. On that day, each Grünherz flyer sensed that the comradeship between the pilots and men of the ground crew had paid off handsomely.

From the beginning of the war up until the 19th of February 1943 the Geschwader's units had flown a total of 58,378 sorties in 21,453 missions and logged 64,846 flight hours.

There was a major shakeup in the structure of the Geschwader on 21 February 1943: III/JG 54 and 4 Staffel were exchanged for I Gruppe of Jagdgeschwader 26 and transferred to France, remaining in the West and in the defense of the Reich until the end of the war.

This exchange transfer and operations are covered in later in the section entitled "III/JG 54 in the West." (page 37)

Stemming from the desire to establish a living link from the front lines to the homeland, a sponsorship developed between the Grünherzgeschwader and the Thüringer Büromaschinen-Werk "Mercedes" in Zella-Mehlis. Officials from the Geschwader paid repeated visits to the workers at home, developing close personal ties in the process.

Beginning in the spring of 1943 the weakening of the Eastern Front grew more and more apparent. The Grünherzgeschwader with the two remaining eastern Gruppen (I/JG 54 and II/JG 54) were often pulled out of the northern sector, repeatedly used in both short-term and long-term "assistance" deployments at all the flashpoints of action along the entire Eastern Front. The Geschwader proved themselves to be a "flying fire brigade." Units of the Geschwader made their appearances in Finland, in the central and southern sectors of the front, over the Ukraine and over Crimea as well.

The Grünherz fighters . . .

. . . flew in the spring of 1943 fighter cover for army units in the Vyazma – Orel region.

. . . supported the last large-scale German offensive, "Zitadelle", near Kursk (5 to 15 July 1943) and flew around-the-clock missions at a significant loss to themselves over the retreating forces of the German army near Orel and Kharkov (17 July to 26 August 1943) in the face of the Red Army's counteroffensive.

. . . fought along with IV/JG 54 in the airspace over the Crimean Peninsula during its evacuation (April to May 1943) and over German army units during their retreat from the Ukraine (August 1943 to April 1944).

Aircraft wearing the green heart could be seen at airbases in Orel, Vyazma , Dugino, Bryansk, Shatalovka, Vitebsk, Kiev, Kharkov, Poltava, Mamaya, Orsha, Neval, Vinnitsa, Idritsa, Zhitomir, Wesenberg (Rakvere), Polotsk, Dünaburg and Dorpat.

Major Hans Philipp, former Kommandeur of I/JG 54, was transferred as Kommodore of Jagdgeschwader 1 on 1 April 1943 and replaced by Major Seiler. After nearly three years as a Kommodore in the Grünherzgeschwader, Oberst Hannes Trautloft was called on 5 July 1943 to be "Inspizient Ost" (Inspector East) in the Office of the General der Jagdflieger.

The new Geschwaderkommodore would be Major Hubertus von Bonin.

I Gruppe was hit particularly hard by the bitter losses in the summer of 1943: Major

Seiler was seriously wounded following his 100th victory on 6 July 1943. His successor as Kommandeur of I/JG 54, Major Gerhard Homuth, led the Gruppe for only three days. During his second mission on 3 August 1943 he was reported missing in action. Oberleutnant Hans Götz, commander of 2 Staffel, jumped into the gap as temporary Kommandeur. He was killed in action on 4 August 1943 after his 82nd victory. Oberleutnant Vinzent assumed the vacant Kommandeur's post until the arrival of Hauptmann Nowotny as the new commander on 10 August 1943. Nowotny's 1 Staffel was later led by Oberleutnant Wettstein, Leutnant Wernicke, Leutnant Tegtmeier and Hauptmann Erdmann.

II Gruppe, too, had its losses. It lost its commander, Hauptmann Jung, on 30 July 1943 after his 68th victory in combat with Russian fighters. Major Rudorffer succeeded him on 1 August 1943.

Oberleutnant Beisswenger, Staffelkapitän of 6 Staffel with 152 kills, was reported missing in action on 6 March 1943 after combat with Russian fighters. His replacement was Leutnant Ademeit.

The Staffelkapitän of 5 Staffel, Oberleutnant Stotz, a victor in 189 dogfights, was forced to bale out on 19 August 1943 after being shot by Russian fighters over Vitebsk and became listed as missing. The Staffel was taken over by Leutnant Wöhnert and later by Leutnant Schleinhege until the war's end.

Despite all these losses, the fighting spirit of the Geschwader remained unbroken.

On 17 July 1943 Feldwebel Missner scored the 5000th victory of the Geschwader, and on 9 October 1943 Hauptmann Nowotny made the 6000th kill.

Hauptmann Nowotny, Kommandeur of I Gruppe, was awarded the Swords on 22 September 1943 after 218 personal kills – and a few days later, on 19 October 1943, was the first pilot of the Geschwader to receive the Diamonds to the Knight's Cross, following his 250th victory.

The Kommodore of the Geschwader, Major Hubertus von Bonin, fell in combat on 15 December 1943 near Orsha. His successor as Kommodore was Oberstleutnant Anton Mader, in January of 1944.

1944

By the beginning of 1944 the initiative in the air war had finally gone over to the Russian Air Force. Enemy aircraft formations appeared in previously unknown masses and were always superior in numbers to the German Luftwaffe. The total strength of all German Jagdgeschwader operating on the Eastern Front was roughly 350 fighters at the beginning of 1944, while the Russians operated ten times as many. The total Soviet aircraft production for 1944 amounted to over 40,000!

I/JG 54, operating with Luftflotte 6 in the central sector of the front, and II/JG 54 with Luftflotte 4 in the southern sector both were pulled back together with the Geschwaderstab into the northern sector, thereby returning once again to Luftflotte 1.

On 4 February 1944 the Kommandeur of I/JG 54, Hauptmann Nowotny, was transferred to Germany in order to establish a "Düsenjägerkommando Me 262."

His replacement was Hauptmann Ademeit, wearer of the Oak Leaves; however, he was forced to land behind enemy lines near Dünaburg on 8 August 1944 after being hit in the engine and became missing in action.

Ademeit's successor was Hauptmann Eisenach, who led I/JG 54 until the end of the war.

Ademeit's former 6 Staffel was taken over by Leutnant Wolf on 4 February 1944, who scored the Geschwader's 7000th victory on 23 March 1944. Leutnant Wolf fell after being hit by flak near Pleskau on 2 April 1944 with 144 kills. The 6 Staffel was then commanded by Leutnant "Bazi" Sterr and later – after reorganization – by Oberleutnant Wettstein until the war's end.

The 3 Staffel of Hauptmann Eisenach was led up until the end of the war by Leutnant Tegtmeier, Leutnant Wernitz and Oberleutnant Eberwein.

II/JG 54 was once again assigned to Finland for a short period, operating from the bases at Helsinki, Petäjärvi and Immola and subordinated to Gefechtverband Kuhlmey. The Gruppe played a successful role in the defensive battles of the Karelian Peninsula lasting several weeks.

With the begin of the Russian summer offensive in June of 1944 the units of Heeresgruppe Nord pulled back under Soviet pressure in a slow and orderly manner via Riga (given up on 13 October 1944) into the Courland region.

Jagdgeschwader 54 followed the army's movements over airfields familiar from the days of the advance into Russia: Dünaburg, Wesenberg, Dorpat, and Riga. In doing so, they permitted the Heer to vacate its sectors according to plan.

At the end of September 1944 the Geschwaderstab and II/JG 54 arrived at the Libau-Grobin airfield, with I/JG 54 arriving at Cirava in Courland beginning near the end of October 1944. Here there was yet another change in the Geschwader leadership structure. In place of the reassigned Oberstleutnant Mader, Oberst Dieter Hrabak (the former Kommandeur of II/JG 54) returned back to the Geschwader on 1 October 1944 as the latest and last Kommodore of the Grünherz pilots.

Oberleutnant Kittel, commander of 2 Staffel, with his 230 aerial victories became the third pilot of the Geschwader to be awarded the Diamonds to the Knight's Cross on 25 November 1944.

On 15 October 1944 Oberleutnant Wettstein, Kapitän of the newly established 6 Staffel, scored the 9000th victory of the Geschwader.

Major Rudorffer, with 210 victories, was the fourth pilot of the Grünherzgeschwader to be recognized with the Swords to the Knight's Cross on 25 January 1945. Rudorffer had been shot down sixteen times himself and had taken to his 'chute nine of those times!

Last Operations in the Courland Pocket

1945

In the tightest of spaces, with their backs to the Baltic Sea, the Grünherz pilots battled out their last duel in the spring of 1945. The Geschwaderstab, I and II Gruppe fought during the six great Courland battles until capitulation on 8 May 1945. There would be no seventh battle in the Courland pocket.

Within a salient of just 150 km diameter and a front of approximately 250 kilometers, the Grünherz fighters fought along with the soldiers of the Kurlandarmee, bravely and with much sacrifice fending off the Soviet deluge both on the ground and in the air.

The pilots flew their missions against a crushing numerical superiority from their bases in Libau-Grobin, Cirava, Tukums, Skunda, Sabile and Windau (Ventspils), beating back enemy bomber and attack formations.

Again and again, the Grünherz fighters were utilized as protection for the supply convoys of the Navy traversing the Baltic, for escorting attack aircraft and for engaging Russian tanks. There were no more German bomber units left in the Courland pocket. The shortage of fuel became the overriding problem of the Geschwader. Operations were sharply influenced by the fuel shortage. Yet in the time period from 1 January to 8 May 1945 over 400 enemy aircraft were shot down by the Geschwader, thankfully with minimal friendly losses.

Among those pilots already considered successful, such as Hrabak, Rudorffer, Eisenach, Thyben, Wettstein, Schleinhege, Broch, Wöhnert, Cordes, Wernitz, Unterlechner, Tegtmeier, etc., Leutnant Kittel demonstrated particular ability. With his 269 victories the most successful pilot of the Geschwader fell on 14 February 1945 in combat while protecting his Army comrades from encirclement.

It was during this time that the pilots of the Grünherzgeschwader were given an unsolicited compliment during the interrogation of a Russian fighter pilot who had been shot down. The Soviet pilot stated: "In battle, the fighters with the green hearts are generally in the minority. But when they're there, things really heat up. They're all aces!"

Only the most critical of the "black men" were permitted into the Courland pocket. The rest were transferred to the airfields at Heiligenbeil (II/JG 54) and Neuhausen (I/JG 54) in East Prussia as Geschwader reserve detachments. Major Rugenstein was leader of the detachments. Replacement aircraft for the Staffeln were transported to the Courland pocket via these two detachments.

During the course of the defensive fighting in East Prussia the soldiers of these detachments were also assigned to Luftwaffe field units or Army units for ground operations. Many of them fell in combat near the town of Pillau.

Capitulation

On 7 May 1945 the commander-in-chief of the Kurlandarmee, Generaloberst Hilpert, offered to capitulate to the Russians. Heeresgruppe Kurland laid down their arms on 8 May 1945. At that time it was the only German Heeresgruppe in a sharply contested front.

During the night of 7-8 May 1945 the last Kommodore of the Grünherzgeschwader, Oberst Hrabak, received a telephone call from the commander of Luftflotte 1, Generaloberst Pflugbeil, with the message: "The German Wehrmacht has capitulated. Flying components of the Geschwader are to return to the Reich under the leadership of the Kommodore at dawn, with the destination of Flensburg. Transport aircraft will be arriving from Norway to pick up the ground personnel – as far as this is possible – beginning at daybreak. Equipment is to be destroyed. Options of using the Marine to evacuate personnel are to be exploited. This commander will remain in Courland and become a Russian prisoner of war."

The two Jagdgruppen were immediately apprised of the situation by the Kommodore and communications were established with the Marine. The unit had quite good relations with this branch of service for mutual benefits, and this now paid off. Ground columns set out on their march to the harbor in Libau.

Home to Germany

The final chapter in the history of Jagdgeschwader 54 is the return flight and transport of the Geschwader remnants from the Courland pocket to Flensburg following the capitulation on 8 May 1945. The Geschwader's ground personnel, along with I and II/JG 54, were able to make it back to Flensburg using the Navy's ships, transport aircraft and even their own Fw 190 fighters. During the transport return, Russian bombing raids on 8 May 1945 against the airfield and harbor of Libau caused considerable losses.

In order to carry the technical personnel in the single-seat Fw 190, the mechanics attached drop tanks and removed superfluous, heavy equipment from the airplanes during the night. In doing so, it ensured that each pilot could "stash" at least two to three "black men" in the aircraft's fuselage for the long flight from the salient over the Baltic to Flensburg.

In Rotten and Schwärme the Grünherz pilots took off before noon on the 8th of May 1945 for their last flight to Flensburg, where approximately 200 personnel from the Geschwader's reserve detachments were already waiting. Under orders, these soldiers had fought their way out of East Prussia beginning in January of 1945 to Schleswig-Holstein via Pillau, Stolp, Prenzlau, Güstrow, Lübeck, and Kiel.

It was during this return journey to Germany on 8 May 1945 that Oberleutnant Thyben, the Staffelkapitän of 4 Staffel, scored the final victory of the Grünherzgeschwader when he shot down a Pe-2 reconnaissance aircraft over the Baltic Sea west of Libau. Curiously, not only was his wingman Fritz Hangebrauck an eyewitness to this, but his crew chief, Albert Mayers could also confirm this as he was stowed in the fuselage of Thyben's Fw 190.

The last of the Grünherz pilots to take off in the late morning hours of 8 May 1945 from the Courland pocket to Germany were Heino Cordes (Staffelkapitän of 2 Staffel), Arthur Lotz, Hans Gött and Oskar Renner.

Internment

As they landed in Flensburg the Grünherz pilots were taken into custody by British soldiers. The reception was not harsh, and initially their sidearms were not even taken from them.

A few days after the arrival of the pilots the bulk of the ground personnel showed up after having been packed to overflowing onto the boats and ships of the Kriegsmarine. Their route took them from the Courland pocket via Kiel and on to Flensburg.

In accordance with an Allied order all German soldiers were to be interned in Schleswig-Holstein, in the region between the Eider and the North Sea canal. A column of approximately 13,000 men wended their way from Flensburg into this area; among them were the men of the "Grünherzgeschwader." Odderade was designated as the "home base" for the Geschwader. In the process, the soldiers of Austrian descent (II/JG 54) were separated from the Geschwader and placed into a special camp. In neighboring Süderhastedt, the remaining personnel of III/JG 54 under Major Klemm could also be found.

Disbandment of the Grünherzgeschwader

Prior to the final release actions, the Geschwader met in Odderade for its final formation. The Kommodore, Oberst Hrabak, disbanded the Geschwader with a brief speech.

By the end of September 194 all Geschwader members had been released.

The "Grünherzgeschwader" had ceased to exist.

This Was Russia!

For nearly four years, from 22 June 1941 to 8 May 1945, the Gruppen, Staffeln, Schwärme and Rotten flew in every season over a land which had previously been alien to the majority of pilots. The vastness of the Russian territory could be felt by the members of the Geschwader from the very first day. It took one's breath away at first. As he crossed the border, each person knew that everything which had happened before would only be a precursor to the most unforgiving conflict in the history of the world. It was rare for a Geschwader during the course of the war to fight so long from one place and from that place to become so familiar with a front region of such dimensions and such movements.

Fall in Russia began early. September brought the first frost. The broad moors in the north, which swallowed up any shot-down or crash-landed airplane, alternately froze up and thawed again until they finally became solid for months on end.

Along with October generally came the first snows. Snow in unimaginable, smothering quantities, then the frost! The men of the Geschwader had come to grips with the land even before the first horrible Russian winter of 1941-1942 clutched the front in its icy grasp and sapped the blood warmth from soldiers to the point where it flickered like a dying ember. In the biting cold tools froze to the clenched hands of the "black men", and yet they continued to work.

Under the expert direction of a Russian senior lieutenant by the name of Kulakoff, who "flew over" to the Grünherz pilots from Leningrad in a "Rata" together with his wife, the snow covered airfields had to be trampled down or rolled smooth – taxiways, takeoff and landing strips – a job which robbed a man's strength to the point of collapse. The men's breath froze and fell to the ground as hoarfrost.

In the dispersal areas of the Staffeln, cumbersome vehicles were replaced with the smaller, more maneuverable horse-drawn Panje sleds.

In the air, the pilots found that their windscreens froze solid despite cockpit heating, so that they had to lean their faces – thickly smeared with anti-frost cream – out at an angle from the open canopies and brave the daggers of the ice storm.

The Soviets flew, and so did the Grünherz fighters.

The Geschwader's pilots fought for their threatened Army comrades above the pock-marked landscape. They attacked ground targets by flying as low as possible – down to the height of the snow-covered trees – then flew escort mission at high altitudes for friendly aircraft; they shot down planes and were themselves shot down. Many a Grünherz pilot crash landed with his engine shot out, landing behind the front lines in a frosty white loneliness, thrust into a cold white hell. Then he took up his rucksack and emergency provisions and, like a peddler or explorer with crucifixes, icons and salt as exchange articles for warmth, shelter and directions, made his way back as best he could, night and day, through endless forests and plains which disappeared into the grayness of the horizon. The Grünherz fighters, in the meantime, waited anxiously at their airbases for the return of their missing comrades, knowing that not all would make it back to their Staffeln.

The roadways will never be forgotten; they have been impressed indelibly into the memory of every Grünherz flyer. With their stoic directness they became representative of the war itself and its incessant to and fro action, first to the East and later back to the West. Roads, unrelenting, stretching over hundreds and hundreds of kilometers, featureless unwavering highways. Roads, brutal like the thongs of a whip, Russian highways which were painful even when viewed from the pilot's cockpit, but even more so when one had to march along them in the summer or winter.

In the spring, the Russian lakes and rivers began thawing and the ice sounded like cannon fire as it burst and crashed together. The sun grew in brightness and the airfields of the Geschwader became transformed into a quagmire of primeval mud, holding fast the fur-lined boots of the pilots as they attempted to laboriously and tortuously move about. When the spring came, and the moors opened up with an eerie silence, and then began the struggle with the filth.

But even then the Geschwader with the green heart continued to fly.

Spring, seeming to blossom abruptly, was shortly followed by the brutally hot, dry summers that changed the earth into fine dust. Sheer walls of dust, kicked up by the wheels and boots, could be seen everywhere along the roads and at the airbases. At the front, they became mixed in with the explosions of the bombs and shells and climbed upward into the super-bright light of the sun. For a brief period the desolate, monotonous gray-green expanses, which could dampen even the strongest of spirits, took on a different color. The forests were given a darker hue, yet even this darkness wasn't a pure green. The dangerous swamps appeared as brownish-green ponds, which confused a crash landing pilot's view down to the lowest altitudes. Even the bushes growing in these marshes were deceptive, while here and there a pool of water, ranging in size from a puddle to a true lake reflecting the dust filled skies, deceived the true nature of the land.

In the high summers of the northern Eastern Front there was seldom a single night's rest. The sun shone for 20 hours straight, and the Grünherzgeschwader flew round the clock.

Whereas the pilot who made a crash landing in winter had to deal with frost, snow and the hardships of the return journey, in summer he was now forced to bear with mosquito swarms, swamps, impenetrable forests and partisans lying in wait everywhere.

The circle of camaraderie within the Grünherzgeschwader among pilots and the "black men" of the ground crew grew closer and closer during the rigors of the Russian seasons and the severity of the fighting.

III/JG 54 in the West

The total reassignment of the Grünherzgeschwader from the Eastern Front to the West in exchange with Jagdgeschwader 26, planned by the General der Jagdflieger in the winter of 1942, was only carried out in part in February of 1943 and eventually given up completely. III/JG 54 under Major "Seppl" Seiler and 4 Staffel under the command of Oberleutnant Graf Matuschka, deployed from Smolensk and Krasnogvardeysk by rail and minus their aircraft to Vendeville near Lille, where they arrived on 12 February 1943. These units would not return to the Eastern Front. III/JG 54 was initially operated as an independent unit flying the Bf 109; later the Gruppe and 4 Staffel were subordinated to Jagdgeschwader 26.

Commanders of III/JG 54 in February 1943 at Vendeville were as follows:

Kommandeur:	Major Seiler
Staffelkapitän 7 Staffel:	Hauptmann Wübke
Staffelkapitän 8 Staffel:	Hauptmann Fink
Staffelkapitän 9 Staffel:	Hauptmann Bob
Staffelkapitän 4 Staffel:	Oberleutnant Graf Matuschka

In exchange with III/JG 54, I Gruppe of Jagdgeschwader 26 under the command of Major Seifert and 7 Staffel under Hauptmann Mietusch were assigned Fw 190A-2s and transferred to the Eastern Front. After three and a half months of operations, primarily in the central sector of the Eastern Front, the units returned back to the West to their mother units.

Contrary to operations over the Eastern Front, III/JG 54 no longer flew in Rotte and Schwarm strength for air defense operations; more and more the pilots were required to become adjusted to flying in Staffel and Gruppe formations.

The Grünherz fighters of III/JG 54 in the West had to master numerous operational areas and many different roles:

27 March 1943 to 22 June 1943:
Air defense operations for airspace under the control of Luftwaffenbefehlshaber Mitte, extending from Oldenburg, for protection the German coast and hinterlands. On 15 March 1943 Hauptmann Fink and Leutnant Rupp fell in combat. On 15 April Major Seiler was transferred to the Eastern Front to become Kommandeur of I/JG 54; his successor was Major Siegfried Schnell.

23 June 1943 to 14 August 1943:
Air defense operations in the region of Luftflotte 3, operating from Deelen, Schipol, and Arnhem, in protection of the coast and rear areas. It was during this time that the courageous Unteroffizier Pfeifer, former world skiing champion, fell in combat. The Staffelkapitän of 9 Staffel, Hauptmann Bob, was transferred in the summer of 1943 to become Kommandeur of IV/JG 51.

15 August 1943 to 6 June 1944:
Air defense in protection of the German coast and rear areas within the jurisdiction of the Luftwaffenbefehlshaber Mitte. Operations were primarily flown from the airfields at Schwerin, Ludwigslust and Lüneburg.

The command of III/JG 54 in Schwerin:

Kommandeur:	Hauptmann Schnell
7 Staffel:	Oberleutnant Klemm
8 Staffel:	Oberleutnant Patzak
9 Staffel:	Oberleutnant Schilling

On 1 February Hauptmann Schnell was transferred to the Eastern Front as commander of IV/JG 54 in a swap with Hauptmann Sinner.

III/JG 54 was temporarily commanded by Oberleutnant Patzak until the arrival of Hauptmann Sinner, but was killed in action in February of 1944. Hauptmann Sinner was wounded in combat in March of 1944, just a few days after he had arrived, and the Gruppe was therefore turned over to the command of Hauptmann Schroer on 14 March 1944.

8 Staffel, orphaned by Oberleutnant Patzak, was taken over in February 1944 by Oberleutnant Zweigert.

The Gruppe suffered considerable losses during its operations from the bases at Schwerin, Ludwigslust and Lüneburg. Accordingly, they were pulled out of combat for a time for rest and recuperation purposes and transferred from Lüneburg via Landau/Isar to Illesheim. It was here that conversion from the Bf 109 to the Fw 190A-8 took place.

During the transfer to Landau a cargo transport glider carrying the technical personnel of 7 Staffel crashed just after taking off from Lüneburg. 25 dead were recorded.

2 Staffel (from I/JG 54) were withdrawn from operations on the Eastern Front in June 1944 and placed under the command of Leutnant Forbrig of III/JG 54. On 10 August 1944 they were redesignated 12 Staffel in Oldenburg.

In Illesheim there was yet another change of commanders. Hauptmann Schroer was assigned to the Jagdfliegerverbandschule; in his place came Hauptmann Weiss.

7 June 1944 to 4 September 1944:
Operations of III/JG 54 on the invasion front within the region of Luftflotte 3, operating from Villacoublay. Missions: support of the Heer through free-ranging fighter sweeps, fighter-bomber strikes, strafing attacks on the enemy's advance and supply columns, plus reconnaissance flights. During the enemy advance the Gruppe withdrew through northern France and Belgium back into German territory. Operational areas of III/JG 54 during the invasion were the Orne estuary, Lisieux, Caen, Evreux, Avranches.

Command positions in Villacoublay at the start of the invasion:

Kommandeur:	Hauptmann Robert Weiss
7 Staffel:	Oberleutnant Fred Teumer
8 Staffel:	Oberleutnant Eugen Zweigert
9 Staffel:	Hauptmann Emil "Bully" Lang
2 Staffel:	Leutnant Horst Forbrig

With over 100 aerial victories the Grünherz pilots of III Gruppe were the most successful of all Jagdgruppen operating over the invasion front.

They were, however, forced to concede serious losses to the numerically superior British and American fighter pilots. After two weeks of operations on the invasion front only four to five pilots per Staffel were combat ready, from the 80 pilots in the Gruppe. It was rare that a young pilot would achieve any more than six missions.

Among those who fell in combat on the invasion front were Oberleutnant Zweigert (10 June 1944) and Leutnant Forbrig (13 June 1944). Hauptmann Lang was reassigned as Kommandeur of II Gruppe in Jagdgeschwader 26 on 25 July 1944.

In mid-June 1944 a heavy American bomber raid struck at the airbase of Villacoublay. Extensive damage occurred, particularly among the equipment and aircraft in the Werftzug and the dispersal area of 7 Staffel.

5 September 1944 to 11 April 1945:

After the serious bloodletting on the invasion front III/JG 54 was transferred to the war front at home to Oldenburg for rest and recuperation. Conversion to the Fw 190 Dora ("Langnasen-Focke") took place there. The Gruppe then operated within the region of Luftflotte Reich in the defense of the Reich. After redesignating the Staffeln and establishing a further Staffel, the following command positions resulted in Oldenburg:

Kommandeur:	Hauptmann Weiss
9 Staffel:	Oberleutnant Heilmann
10 Staffel:	Leutnant Prager
11 Staffel:	Leutnant Crump (Hauptmann Bottländer)
12 Staffel:	Leutnant Dortenmann

The majority of the newly arriving pilots were former, often highly-decorated, but generally older bomber pilots, who were to actually have been utilized as Staffelkapitäne within the Gruppe. Their experiences as bomber pilots, however, meant little compared with the different requirements dictated by fighter combat, and for the most part they were simply used as Rotten and Schwarm pilots.

The former commander of the Grünherzgeschwader's I Gruppe, the brilliantly successful Major Walter Nowotny, had established the "Düsenjäger-Erprobungskommando Me 262" (Me 262 Jet Fighter Evaluation Detachment) on 26 September 1944 in Lechfeld. In the first days of October "Kommando Nowotny" and 23 jets transferred to their operational airbases at Hesepe and Achmer near Osnabrück. On 12 October 1944, 9 Staffel/JG 54 under Oberleutnant Heilmann was assigned from Oldenburg to Hesepe and 12 Staffel/JG 54 under Leutnant Dortenmann to Achmer for airfield protection of Nowotny's Me 262s during their landings and takeoffs. Both Staffeln yet again suffered devastating losses in fulfilling this role. On 8 November 1944 Major Nowotny, piloting an Me 262, fell in combat in the immediate vicinity of the airbase. "Kommando Nowotny" was disbanded.

On Christmas Eve 1944 9 and 12 Staffel transferred to Varrelbusch and there once again met up with the remnants of III/JG 54 On 25 December 1944 III/JG 54 was subordinated to JG 26. Operating from Varrelbusch, the Gruppe continued flying over the invasion front in the West and in defense of the Reich.

During these difficult times the commander of III Gruppe, Hauptmann Weiss, had this to say about the exemplary cooperation between officer and NCO pilots: "Other than our lives, we have nothing to lose. Flying will continue. Our NCO pilots will constantly back us up. Even in the deepest mire they won't abandon us!"

On 29 December 1944 the Gruppe, which had already weathered severe trials, saw the blackest day in its history yet. Carrying out an erroneous order by the ground controllers, the Grünherz pilots formed up in Staffeln to attack a vastly superior force of Spitfires in the area of Münster-Osnabrück-Rheine, and once again suffered devastating losses. The proven commander of the Gruppe, Hauptmann Robert Weiss, victor of 121 dogfights, fell in combat while flying at the head of III/JG 54, along with an additional eight pilots; the strength ratio in comparison with enemy fighters was 1:10!

Until the arrival of the new Kommandeur III/JG 54 was temporarily under the command of Oberleutnant Dortenmann and Oberleutnant Heilmann.

On 1 January 1945 III/JG 54, together with I/JG 26, took off from Fürstenau in support of fighter operations for the large-scale "Bodenplatte" operation. Overnight, the trusty "black men" had taken the unit's worn-out and damaged aircraft and made them combat ready again. In the early dawn hours of 1 January 16 pilots of III/JG 54 took off and, flying at treetop height, successfully carried out strikes with their guns against the Grimberghen airbase near Brussels. With Operation "Bodenplatte" there were yet more killed and missing in action. III/JG 54 never completely recovered from these devastating blows.

On 15 February 1945 the new commander arrived in the person of Major Klemm. Command hierarchy of III/Jg 54 until its disbandment on 11 April 1945 was:

Kommandeur:	Major Klemm
9 Staffel:	Oberleutnant Heilmann
10 Staffel:	Leutnant Crump
11 Staffel:	Oberleutnant Dortenmann (later Leutnant Prager)
Stabskompanie:	Hauptmann Neumann
Nachrichtenoffizier:	Hauptmann Funk
Gruppenbeamter:	Oberzahlmeister Rudoff
Sanitätsoffizer:	Oberarzt Dr. Busemeyer

On 25 February 1945 III/JG 54 was redesignated as IV/JG 26 and the Staffeln, too, were given new designations accordingly. In doing so, this respectable Gruppe was removed from Jagdgeschwader 54, yet their home continued to be with the Grünherzgeschwader.

The former Grünherz fighters continued to fly missions with JG 26 in support of the Reich defense. Numerous pilots fell in the last weeks of the war, Leutnant Crump, Leutnant Prager and Oberleutnant Dortenmann being among them.

On 24 March Varrelbusch airbase was flattened by an American four-engine bomber strike; once again the Gruppe was forced to accept losses in personnel and equipment.

On 11 April 1945 the final disbandment of the former III/JG 54 took place in Klein-Kummersfelde. The remaining pilots and a portion of the ground personnel were absorbed into units of Jagdgeschwader 26. A large number of the "black men" were incorporated into the Heer for ground fighting operations.

IV/Jagdgeschwader 54

In July 1943 Hauptmann Erich Rudorffer was ordered to establish a IV Gruppe of the Grünherzgeschwader in Jesau near Königsberg. But just a few days after his arrival in Jesau he was given new orders once again, this time to take over the vacant commander's post of II/JG 54 on the Eastern Front beginning on 1 August 1943.

Hauptmann Rudolf Sinner became the second commander of the Bf 109 equipped IV/JG 54. Under his command, the Gruppe carried the coat-of-arms of the Prince of Savoy. It showed a white stripe with three hedgehogs on a red field.

Later IV Gruppe fell in line with Geschwader tradition and took as its symbol a reference to its place of birth. Since this had occurred near Königsberg, the Gruppe was given permission by the city to utilize a stylized coat-of-arms of the city of Königsberg.

Under Hauptmann Sinner, the pilots initially flew escort missions and fighter sweeps along the Eastern Front's northern sector. The weakening front lines dictated rapid redeployments from Siverskaya to the airfields at Idritsa, Dno, Pleskau and Dorpat. The 12 Staffel was employed as a Jabo Staffel for low-level strikes with bombs and integral guns.

Command structure as of the end of November 1943:

Kommandeur:	Hauptmann Sinner
Kapitän 10 Staffel:	Oberleutnant Deterra
Kapitän 11 Staffel:	Oberleutnant Leykauf
Kapitän 12 Staffel:	Hauptmann Koall
Adjutant:	Leutnant Vermeulen
Hauptmann beim Stabe:	Hauptmann Wilhelm Haase
Technischer Offizier:	Oberleutnant "Jupp" Gröne
Nachrichtenoffizier:	Leutnant "Bazi" Kröll
Waffenoffizier:	Oberfeldwebel Wokasek
Sanitätsoffizier:	Stabsarzt Dr. Ludewig
Chef der Stabskompanie:	Oberleutnant Staschik

Hauptmann Sinner was transferred to III/JG 54 as its commander in February of 1944; his replacement was Hauptmann Siegfried Schnell, who, however, fell in combat on 25 February in the northern sector of the Eastern Front.

In mid-April 1943 the Gruppe deployed from the region of Luftflotte 1 to the southern sector of Luftflotte 4, there providing fighter protection to Heer units retreating out of the Crimea and their disengagement from the Dnjestr front. In fulfilling this role, the pilots used the Rumanian airfields of Mamaia near Constanza (on the Black Sea), Roman and Leipzig (in Bessarabia). During this time the Gruppe was temporarily under the command of Hauptmann Gerhard Koall, whose 12 Staffel was led by Hauptmann "Hein" Wübke.

During the transfer from the northern sector to Mamaia, a distance of nearly 2000 kilometers, the Gruppe ran into bad weather and several aircraft were lost; initially only five of the Gruppe's Bf 109s arrived in Rumania. An advance party of the main technical personnel travelled in two Ju 52 transports, but both transports crashed after being fired upon by long range American fighters over the Danube.

After just a few weeks in operation, the decimated Gruppe was reassigned to Illesheim via Landau (Isar) to convert to the Fw 190A-8.

Here, under the supervision of the new Kommandeur Major Wolfgang Späte, the Gruppe was virtually created anew. The Gruppe was beefed up to four Staffeln, each with 16 aircraft, which brought it up to strength requirements for Reich defense operations. In Illesheim the Gruppe had approximately 80 pilots and 80 Fw 190s.

On 30 June 1944 another set of unexpected orders came down, assigning the Gruppe to the Luftflotte 6 district for air defense and escort operations. The pilots flew mainly fighter sweeps over the fleeing Heer units along the Russo-Polish border areas ranging within the area of Bobruysk-Beresina-Bug. Command structure as of the beginning of July 1944:

Kommandeur:	Major Späte
Kapitän 10 Staffel:	Oberleutnant Klemm
Kapitän 11 Staffel:	Oberleutnant Deterra
Kapitän 12 Staffel:	Oberleutnant Haala
Kapitän 13 Staffel:	Leutnant "Bazi" Sterr

Operational bases within Luftflotte 6 were Baranovichi, Lublin, Deblin, Radom, Modlin, Nasielsk, Lemberg and, on 21 August 1944, Trakehnen. This was the airfield from which the Grünherzgeschwader first took off on 22 June 1941 at the start of the Russian campaign.

From the beginning of July to the beginning of September 1944 the Gruppe lost three of its Staffelkapitäne in operations on the Eastern Front. The commander of 11 Staffel, Oberleutnant Deterra, was killed in a dogfight; his successor, Leutnant Horst Hartrampf, was pulled out dead from his burning aircraft which had just landed at Nasielsk, while the Kapitän of 12 Staffel, Oberleutnant Haala, was shot down in flames by anti-aircraft fire and became a Russian prisoner of war.

The Kommandeur of the Gruppe, Major Späte, had to take to his parachute each time after being shot down twice in combat with the space of a short time.

Although he suffered facial burns, he was quite lucky when Russian fighters fired upon him and missed while he was hanging from his parachute.

At the beginning of September IV/JG 54 was assigned to Reich territory for a short period of rest and recuperation, transferring to the airbases at Zichenau, Löbnitz and eventually Plantlünne. After this period, they operated from Holland against the invasion forces and in the defense of the Reich.

Flying from Plantlünne, the pilots once again operated in large formations in defense of the Reich, carrying out attacks against American four-engine bomber wings.

Within the space of three weeks the Gruppe suffered heavy casualties. They lost over 30 pilots in combat with numerically superior Mustang and Thunderbolt fighters while accounting for only ten kills themselves. IV/JG 54 therefore had to be taken out of action once again, transferring to Mörtitz on 7 October for rest and recuperation.

On 16 October 1944 Major Späte, the Kommandeur of the Gruppe, was assigned to JG 400 as its Kommodore. Hauptmann Rudi Klemm took over the Gruppe as its new commander. Command structure on 1 November 1944:

Kommandeur:	Hauptmann Klemm
Kapitän 13 Staffel:	Hauptmann Brill
Kapitän 14 Staffel:	Leutnant Budde
Kapitän 15 Staffel:	Leutnant Resch
Kapitän 16 Staffel:	Oberleutnant "Bazi" Sterr

The Grünherzgeschwader at this time had been built up to four Gruppen, each with four Staffeln (1 Staffel to 6 Staffel), which explains the new numbering of the Staffeln within IV/JG 54 when compared with July 1944.

After recuperation, Reich defense operations continued from the airbases at Münster-Handorf (19 November 1944) and Vörden (21 November 1944).

IV/JG 54 flew during the Ardennes offensive, over Holland and during the Battle of Arnhem.

On 26 November 1944 the Staffelkapitän of 16 Staffel, Oberleutnant "Bazi" Sterr, was shot down over the airfield perimeter at Vörden while on landing approach. He was an experienced pilot with over 500 combat sorties and 129 victories. Sterr's replacement as Staffel leader, Leutnant Brandt, fell on 24 December 1944 in a dogfight near Münster; a few days later Leutnant Budde, the Staffelkapitän of 14 Staffel, lost his life over the Nürburgring as well.

On 1 January 1945 the pilots participated in the large-scale Luftwaffe operation known as "Bodenplatte." Taking off from Vörden, the pilots conducted a successful strike against the airfield at Brussels-Melsbruck.

Following Operation "Bodenplatte", IV/JG 54 was once again employed in the defense of the Reich.

On 14 January 1945 the remainder of the Gruppe, under the command of 15 Staffel's Leutnant Resch, flew their last mission with 16 pilots taking off from the Vörden airbase. During their attack on an American heavy bomber formation, the Gruppe was practically gutted by numerically superior American escort fighters. Of the 16 Grünherz pilots who had taken off, only two returned – Unteroffizier Walter and Unteroffizier Kempken; 14 pilots had been shot down, ten of them killed in action. Among the latter was Leutnant Resch who, following a crash landing was gunned down by Mustangs while attempting to climb out of his aircraft.

The ten fallen Grünherz pilots found their last resting place in the Damme cemetery.

IV/JG 54 had been bled dry! Its final disbandment took place in February 1945 in Gardelegen. Members of the ground personnel were transferred to II Gruppe of Jagdgeschwader 77.

A second "establishment" of IV/JG 54 in the spring of 1945 was simply a redesignation of II Gruppe of Zerstörergeschwader 76 to IV/JG 54. This renaming and conversion to Fw 190s took place under Hauptmann Schlossstein in Grossenhain. In April 1945 this Gruppe was also disbanded. At no time was it ever directly subordinated to the Grünherzgeschwader.

The Ergänzungsstaffel of the Grünherz Fighters

The Ergänzungstaffel (E/JG 54), generally at some distance from the front, had the task of training those green pilots arriving from the Jagdfliegerschulen in the intricacies of operations within the Grünherzgeschwader on the particular front (Eastern or Western). Training time ranged from six to ten weeks. For this purpose the Staffelkapitän had four to eight experienced fighter pilots available as fighter instructors. These "old hands" were temporarily detached from the front Staffeln to the E/Staffel.

The establishment of E/JG 54 took place in October of 1940 under Oberleutnant Zilken in Bergen (Holland). The first Staffelkapitän was Oberleutnant Eggers.

In November 1940 the E/Staffel transferred to Cazaux, France. Among the instructors for the 20 fighter pilot students at the time were Leutnant Frenzel-Beyme, Oberfeldwebel de Vries, Feldwebel Schildknecht and Feldwebel Windisch.

In the spring of 1941 the E/Staffel in Cazaux was strengthened to an Ergänzungsjagdgruppe with a training and an operational Staffel.

Command hierarchy of E/Gruppe JG 54 on 20 March 1941:

Kommandeur:	Oberleutnant Eggers
1 Staffel (op.):	Oberleutnant Fink
2 Staffel (tng):	Oberleutnant Hörmann
Stabskompanie:	Oberleutnant der Reserve "Papa" Straus

With the beginning of the Russian campaign E/Gruppe JG 54 moved initially to Neukuhren (East Prussia). On 22 May 1941 there were 72 fighter trainees in the two Staffeln.

The young pilots of the operational Staffel flew their first combat missions during the advance into Lithuania, Latvia, Estonia and later in the northern sector of the Eastern Front, where they fought heroically. Operational areas included: Windau, Riga, Pernau, Ösel, Siverskaya and Krasnogvardeysk.

The E/Gruppe suffered a tragic loss while in combat over the island of Ösel. Leutnant Henkemeier was forced to take to his parachute to escape his burning plane. Defenseless, suspended from his 'chute, he was shot to death.

Leutnant Nowotny, who would later become such a successful Grünherz fighter, accomplished an unusual and remarkable feat during this period. After he had been shot down by flak over Ösel (occupied at the time by the Russians) he was forced to ditch his Bf 109 in the sea. Before the airplane sank, however, Nowotny managed to inflate his one-man raft carried in the aircraft. In order not to fall into Russian captivity he paddled an adventurous 60 kilometer journey from Ösel to the distant coast of Estonia, which he finally reached after 52 hours – completely exhausted.

On 9 March 1942 the E/Gruppe in Krasnogvardeysk was disbanded. Personnel and material were distributed among the other Staffeln of the Geschwader. E/Gruppe JG 54 could claim 51 kills to its credit at the time of disbandment.

With the disbandment of the E/Gruppe a newly established Ergänzungsjagdgeschwader assumed training of the new pilots for the entire Jagdwaffe. It was divided into two Ergänzungsgruppen: "West" and "Ost (East)." In both of the Ergänzungsgruppen there were Ergänzungsstaffeln which provided specialized training for specific front-line Geschwader units, to include JG 54. The Grünherzgeschwader provided veteran fighter pilot instructors for this E/Staffeln in the Ergänzungsgruppen "Ost" and "West", to include: Döbele, Ohlsen, Hünherfeld, Brock, Kretschmer, Brill, Frenzel-Beyme, Clerico, Kittel, Hannig, Kroschinski, Raupach, Luer, Cordes, Rademacher, Schilling and Forbrig.

They all played a major role in the training of the young pilots.

The airbases which hosted the fresh pilots for the Grünherzgeschwader were primarily: In the West: Biarritz, Toulouse, Bergerac; In the East: Liegnitz, Rodau-Rosenau, Sagan.

The matter of fighter replacements became more and more critical as the war drew to a close and losses increased.

Under the massive pressure of the enemy the young fighter pilots were sent into combat much too early, on orders of the senior Luftwaffe command. To be sure, they brought with them the highest recommendations and the best of intentions, but without satisfactory front-line experience they generally fell in combat on the first missions against a numerically superior and battle hardened enemy.

Successes

The successes of battles and duels by the army are generally indicated by captured material and numbers of prisoners. With a Jagdgeschwader, however, what counts are the number of kills, its participation in authorized and completed missions escorting friendly bombers, transports, Stukas or reconnaissance aircraft – which cannot be measured in numbers, and finally in equipment destroyed on the ground through low-level attacks.

No less than 9400 enemy aircraft were destroyed by the Grünherz pilots, either on the ground or shot down in air combat.

If these aircraft were to be lined up next to each other wingtip to wingtip they would stretch out for a distance of over 120 kilometers, or roughly the distance from Frankfurt to Würzburg.

In addition to the aircraft destroyed, there were also thousands of strafing and fighter-bomber attacks resulting in the destruction of countless trucks, transports, locomotives, tanks, tethered balloons, anti-aircraft and artillery positions, ships and weapons of every kind.

Along with the repeated mention of the Grünherzgeschwader and its successful, highly decorated pilots in Wehrmacht reports, in the press and on radio, throughout the war appreciatory letters addressed to the Geschwader and its subordinate units were constantly arriving at the command post from the highest Luftwaffe and Heer commands.

The Grünherz fighters were particularly pleased with the recognition paid by their army comrades, ranging from a telex from the Oberbefehlshaber der Heeresgruppe Nord to a hand scribbled and smudged scrap of paper with the thanks of a company commander from his foxhole in the Volkhov pocket.

The thank you messages for safe escort of the bombers, a role which the Grünherz pilots always carried out with circumspection and attentiveness, were a constant source of welcome news.

Two letters of recognition are provided here as an example for all those received.

The Oberbefehlshaber der Heeresgruppe Nord, Generaloberst von Küchler, transmitted the following telex to the Kommodore of the Grünherzgeschwader on the occasion of its 2,000th aerial victory:

"I would like to express to you and your Jagdgeschwader 54 my most sincere congratulations and recognition for the 2,000th kill on 4 April 1942.

By far, the greatest percentage of these victories were scored by the Jagdgeschwader in the combat arena of Heeresgruppe Nord! With this, your Jagdgeschwader has not only secured an eternal place in the annals of Luftwaffe history, but it has also been a never-to-be discounted example of aid and support in the true spirit of camaraderie to the Heer in many difficult battles. My best wishes for continued successes and may the fortunes of war accompany you and your brave Geschwader!

von Küchler, Generaloberst"

During an escort mission for an He 111 bomber formation Feldwebel "Quax" Schnörrer, a friend and wingman to Walter Nowotny, provided safe passage against brutal attacks by Russian fighters for a heavily shot-up He 111. He escorted the crippled bomber over a distance of 60 kilometers until crossing over friendly lines. The pilot of the He 111, Oberfeldwebel Jan Recke, thanked him and later sent "Quax" Schnörrer a photo with the message:

"To my friend Karl Schnörrer, who saved the lives of me and my crew on the 5th of June 1943 during an attack on the locks at Novo Ladoga, in thanks. Karl gave us 20 minutes' time and successfully protected us from the attacks of Russian fighters until the crash landing of our He 111, shot by flak, behind the German lines."

Frau Recke added:

"Dear Herr Schnörrer, I, too, would like to thank you with all my heart for keeping our Daddy safe.

With best wishes, Frau Recke and little Helga."

With 267 kills, Oberleutnant Otto Kittel was the most successful fighter of the Grünherzgeschwader. He was followed by Major Walter Nowotny with 250, Major Erich Rudorffer with 222 and Hans Philipp with 206 victories.

20 pilots in the Geschwader scored over 100 victories, 58 pilots over 50 and 114 pilots over 20 kills.

The last authentic situational report of the Geschwader, from 31 December 1944, contained among other things a listing of the successes of the individual Stäbe, Gruppen and Staffeln. According to the report, as of 31 December 1944 (i.e. four months before the end of the war) the Grünherzgeschwader had tallied 9,141 aerial victories, of which 8,502 were in the East. The remaining situational reports continuing up to the capitulation on 8 May 1945 have all been lost.

However, as a result of exhaustive research the total successes of the Geschwader to the war's end can be provided with some degree of accuracy. This research indicates the total number of kills to be at least 9,400, probably even higher.

Two units primarily operating in the East had the greatest amount of kills, I/JG 54 with 3,564 and II/JG 54 with 3,621. III/JG 54 attained 1,500 and IV/JG 54 had a total of 550 air victories.

165 kills were scored by the pilots of the Geschwaderstab of JG 54 and 51 by E/JG 54.

The successes of the pilots of III/JG 54 and IV/JG 54 were somewhat lower in the West and during the Reich defense because they were forced to fight under significantly harsher conditions during the last months of the war.

A comparison of the successes and losses of the Geschwader illustrates the fighting conditions prevalent at the time:

Unit	**Victories**	**Total Losses** *(KIA, fatal crashes, and MIA)*	
		Pilots	**Ground Personnel**
Stab JG/54	44	1	1
I/JG 54	920	37	2
II/JG 54	952	40	5
III/JG 54	221	100	12
IV/JG 54	476	82	30
Total	2,613	260	50

Losses

The years of tough operations didn't pass without leaving their mark on the Geschwader. Many casualties were suffered both in the ranks of the pilots as well as among soldiers of the ground crew, but even the suffering of the Grünherz fighters had its limits.

The total number of dead and missing are not precisely known due to the fact that all war records and official documents have been lost. The figure is likely to be around 1,000, of which 600 alone were pilots. Which means that the personnel strength in pilots turned over five times and had to be filled out with replacement pilots.

Just of the 68 Grünherz pilots who were awarded with various degrees of the Knight's Cross, 47 of them were either killed, went missing in action, or died as a result of the war.

These painful losses affected all ranks of service, from the Geschwaderkommodore down to the lowliest Fliegersoldat. The Staffelkapitäne and Kommandeure, who flew at the front of their formations, had to pay a particularly high price in blood. They literally died at the head of their men.

The percentage of officers and officer cadets who were killed in action was 35 percent.

The pilots generally died in aerial combat or were shot down by flak or other anti-aircraft weapons. Other pilots were killed during post-maintenance flights, in poor weather, or during takeoffs and landings.

The highest losses suffered by the pilots were borne by III and IV Gruppe in the defense of the Reich and during the Normandy invasion.

The men of the ground personnel suffered the majority of their losses during enemy bombing attacks on our airfields, when their transport planes crashed, during redeployments when under fire from enemy fighters and ground-based guns, in partisan raids, in accidents and, toward the end of the war, in ground fighting.

Afterword

The memories of the Grünherzgeschwader will continue to be kept alive in our Luftwaffe. The proven Jagdgeschwader 34 has assumed the traditional rights to Jagdgeschwader 54 and in doing so, has provided the Grünherz fighters a lasting "support base" in Memmingen.

In a ceremony on the 26th of November 1982 former Kommodore Hannes Trautloft passed the Grünherz coat of arms to the (then) Kapitän of 1 Jagdbomberstaffel, Major Detlef Scharf and stated:

> "May this coat of arms become a solid tie between old and young pilots, and may it also be a challenge to consider the history which has gone before, gain new courage and dare to believe in a peaceful future!"

With this legacy, 1 Jagdbomberstaffel became the Traditionsstaffel of the old Jagdgeschwader 54. Since then, the pilots wear the Grünherz coat of arms combined with the symbol of the Staffel as a visible sign of their alliance and camaraderie. This insignia, worn on the flying suits of the young pilots in Memmingen, also represents a visible unity with an unforgettable, formerly blossoming part of our Fatherland. The tradition of the Grünherzgeschwader will continue to live on among the men of 1 Staffel of Jagdgeschwader 34 long after the last Grünherz fighter has taken off on his last flight.

Every two years the members of two flyer generations and their families meet together for a combined Geschwader gathering at the airbase in Memmingen.

They come from all over to this great "family reunion." From Austria, from "over there" in Thuringia or even, as Gerhard Thyben, from distant Colombia.

This is no gathering of a beer-drinking soldiers' or military club. There is something there which goes beyond camaraderie, something which can't be accurately defined and can't be confused with camaraderie. It is the purely human relationship of one with another, the knowledge that one can completely rely upon another with whom he has gone through both thick and thin.

This feeling of togetherness has never become undermined among the Grünherz fighters, nor has it ever vanished or become blurred.

To be sure, they have all changed in their external appearances, but they all are still on the same frequency!

When the Grünherz fighters shake hands, they can sense what the great and sensitive pilot and author Antoine de Saint Exupéry meant when he said:

> "One only sees well with the heart. The important things are invisible to the eye."

JG 54
Grunherzjäger Photo Section

A parade on the occasion of the formation of Jagdgruppe Wien-Aspern in April 1938. The Jagdgruppe Wien-Aspern was created from 1 and 2 Staffel of the former Austrian Jagdgeschwader 2, as well as 3 Staffel and the Stabskompanie (headquarters company) of Jagdgruppe Bad Aibling. Hauptmann von Müller-Riensburg reviews the front row of the newly arrived personnel formation together with Hauptmann Gärtner and Leutnant Hrabak.

Leutnant Philipp and Leutnant Bielefeld are the flag officers, seen with the newly presented Gruppe flag.

Vienna-Aspern airbase. Officers of I/JG 76, later to become II Gruppe of Jagdgeschwader 54. From left to right: Brustellin, Gärtner, Ewald, Maculan, Mader, and von Müller-Riensburg.

Group photo of 3 Staffel I/JG 76 – later 6 Staffel with Staffelkapitän Oberleutnant Eckerle. Summer 1939.

This He 51 found itself on its back after its final flight, just before converting over to the Bf 109D and Fiat CR-32.

III/JG 54 was formed from I Gruppe of JG 21. The peacetime sites of this Gruppe were in Jesau and Gutenfeld in eastern Prussia. This photo was taken on 17 July 1939 in front of the mess in Gutenfeld and shows (from left): Kommandeur Major Mettig, Schön, Rödel, Scholz, Schneider, Eggers, Dress, ?, Schelcher.

The maintenance crew of 3 Staffel with a plaque which reads: "Avia – Jagdarena – 1939" in Herzogenaurach.

Herzogenaurach near. Nuremberg. The Franconian area was home to the I/JG 70, which became I/JG 54 on 15 September 1939. During the early summer the Gruppe was given the task of evaluating Czech-designed Avia planes. The Bf 109D was also put through its paces by the unit.

Prior to the beginning of the Polish campaign I/JG 76 (later II/JG 54) and I/JG 21 (later III/JG 54) deployed to airfields in East Prussia, Silesia and Czechoslovakia. This photo was taken in August of 1939 at the Stubendorf airfield and shows (from left to right): Leutnant von Aspern (white shirt), Leutnant Bielefeld, Hauptmann von Müller-Riensburg, Oberleutnant Hrabak, Oberleutnant der Reserve Seibt and Oberleutnant Mader.

Only II and III Gruppe took part in the Polish campaign. At the time, both Gruppen were still equipped with the Bf 109D. Right photo: aircraft of the "Teufelsstaffel" (Devil's Staffel, 9 Staffel) dispersed at an airfield in East Prussia.

Prior to the outbreak of hostilities Poland had a total of 396 aircraft, many of which were destroyed on the ground by strafing attacks. The Polish PZL 11c was markedly inferior to the Bf 109D.

A Staffel dispersal area of III Gruppe in East Prussia.

Soon the first Iron Crosses 2nd Class (EK 2) were being awarded. In Rostken, East Prussia, a bottle is opened in keeping with an old pilot's custom. From left: Kommandeur Major Mettig, Leutnant Rödel, Leutnant Schön, and Leutnant Lange.

A relaxed group photo of I/JG 21 (III/JG 54) following the end of the Blitzkrieg. From left to right: Lange, Eggers, Müller, Schmidt, Eberle, Wacker, Behrens, Major Mettig, Schneider, Scholz, Schmidt, Toni Schmidt, Hausmann, and Strauss.

Toothaches can be particularly bothersome. Here, the unit dentist is seen in action with his portable, foot-operated drill. Dieter Hrabak resigns himself willingly to his unavoidable fate.

Following the end of hostilities in Poland all three Gruppen occupied airbases in Western and Southern Germany. Here, components of the future II Gruppe have found refuge in the large Zeppelin hangar in Rhein-Main.

Ground personnel and drivers of the future II/JG 54 during mealtime and seen preparing sumptuous food to order.

I/JG 54, which remained in Herzogenaurach for the duration of the Polish campaign, was now transferred to the airfields in Böblingen, Friedrichshafen and Eutingen bei Horb. The Zeppelin hangar in Friedrichshafen also provided shelter for fighters, bombers and Stukas.

The Kapitän of 1 Staffel, "Seppl" Seiler, is seen high in the saddle at the Eutingen airfield.

The winter sportsmen of 3 Staffel arrived in Böblingen fully prepared.

On 3 February 1940 the Kommandeur of I/JG 21, Major Mettig, bade farewell to his troops in Mönchengladbach. He then went on to become the Kommodore of Jagdgeschwader 54.

The Gruppe was then placed under the command of Hauptmann Ultsch.

May's first days in Mönchengladbach were so nice that it was possible to dine outdoors. The photo shows (from outer left): Lange, Ostermann, Heinbockel, Dress; (end of table): Schmidt (admin.), Ultsch, Schelcher, Scholz; (outer right): Strauss, Neumann; (inner seating from left): Eggers, Baumgärtner, Busse, Leutnant Schmidt.

I Gruppe flew its first operations with their new Bf 109Es against France from Eutingen. One of the Gruppe's maintenance tents is seen in the background.

An impressive photo showing a Rotte taking off, just before lifting free of the ground.

The "dicky-bird" seen on the engine housing of this aircraft was the symbol of 8 Staffel.

One of 8 Staffel's airfields in France. The first kill markings can be seen on the airplane rudders quite clearly. The middle "Emil" with the large "3" was flown by Leutnant Erwin Leykauf.

Several pilots of 3 Staffel were awarded the Iron Cross 2nd Class (EK 2) following a successful low-level attack on the French airfield of Luxeuil. From rear left: Unteroffizier Kranz, Oberleutnant Schmoller-Haldy (Staffelkapitän), Leutnant Kinzinger, Leutnant Angeli, Leutnant Witt. Front: Unteroffizier Windisch, Feldwebel Knedler.

A few pilots of 8 Staffel in Signy-le-Petit were also presented with the EK 2. Center: Leutnant Behrens, Leutnant Lange, Leutnant Ostermann, Feldwebel Clerico.

A component of the Funkzug (Communications platoon) in the Western campaign.

During the Western campaign II Gruppe was led by Major Kraut (5 February to 10 July 1940). He was succeeded by Hauptmann Winterer, who commanded up until 14 August 1940.

Self-service by the Stabskompanie procured fresh milk near Abbeville.

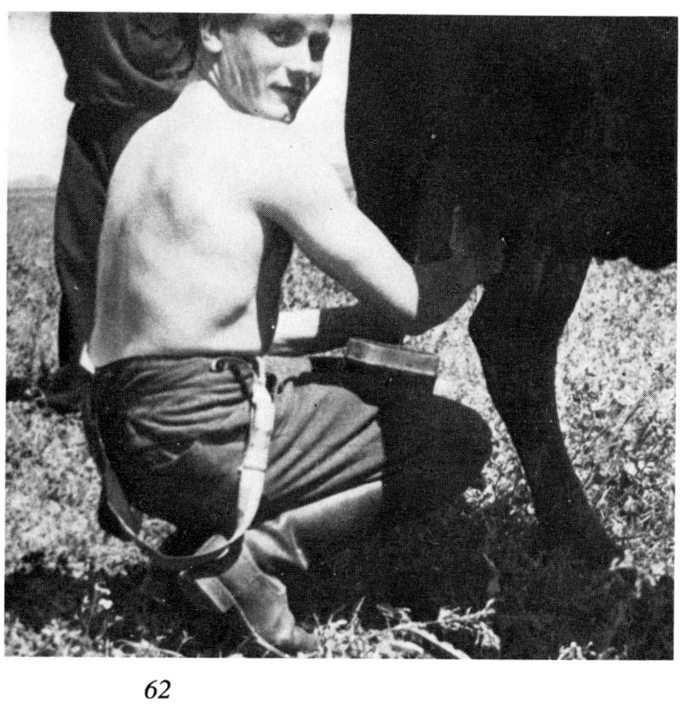

A captured British flag flutters from the Staffelwagen of 9 Staffel (Teufelsstaffel).

In June of 1940 the first Iron Crosses 1st Class (EK 1) were awarded to successful pilots by the Kommandeur of II Gruppe, Major Kraut. These are (from left): Oberleutnant Hrabak, Leutnant Philipp, and Oberfeldwebel Stotz.

Because of the rapid advances by the German ground forces, the Luftwaffe was generally able to occupy airfields in France, Holland, and Belgium almost immediately.

Leutnant Hans Philipp, Kapitän of 4 Staffel, demonstrated his outstanding flying abilities as early as his first combat sorties. He soon became numbered among the aces of the German Jagdwaffe. His "Emil" carried his personal symbol, a magician magically making the enemy's airplanes disappear from the skies.

This photo with a windmill may have been taken in De Kooey, Holland. "Red 13" of the Teufelsstaffel provides a picturesque complement to the landscape.

The Werftzug (Maintenance platoon) of I Gruppe's Stabskompanie caught during one of its numerous moves, here in front of a Ju 52 transport.

Airfield alert at 3 Staffel in Groningen, Holland. Here, life jackets were a standard part of a pilot's apparel.

The trailer of 9 Staffel not only showed all the countries through which it had travelled, it was also a victory scoreboard for the unit.

During the Battle of Britain, the Geschwader's Gruppen were stationed at airfields near Calais; the Geschwaderstab and I Gruppe were in Campagne, II Gruppe in Harlinghem (later Campagne), and III Gruppe in Guines (photo).

Group photo of the Geschwaderstab in August 1940 at the Channel. From left to right: Oberleutnant Lange (Geschwader-Adjutant), Kommodore Major Mettig, KFZ-Offizier Reymann, and Hauptmann Vollath.

Generaloberst Milch visits the Geschwaderstab in Guines in August of 1940. In conjunction with the rejuvenation of the Geschwader leadership, Major Hannes Trautloft assumed command of Jagdgeschwader 54 on 25 August 1940. The photo shows (from left to right): Generaloberst Milch, Major Mettig, Leutnant Neumann.

There was a change of commanders in II Gruppe as well. On 14 August Hptm. Winterer turned the Gruppe over to Oblt. Hrabak, who led it from 26 August 1940 until 27 October 1942. (Oblt. Hrabak, left, and Hptm. Winterer in the Gruppe's command post)

Fw. Hier was joyfully welcomed at the Rotterdam airfield after being returned from a French prisoner-of-war camp. Hier was later reported missing in action on 15 November 1940 following a sortie over London. On 7 December 1940 he was found washed up on the Dutch coast, dead. From left to right: Lt. Ziegler, Hptm. Hrabak, Fw. Hier, Lt. Schypek.

Leutnant Bob from 9 Staffel shot down his 10th enemy on 18 August 1940 near Calais. The British pilot was fortunately able to bellyland his plane, however. (Leutnant Bob is third from left.)

Group photo of the "heavy hitters" of I Gruppe. From left: Hauptfeldwebel Kröger, Feldwebel Baukes, Hauptfeldwebel Seliger, Hauptfeldwebel Stiller.

Captured British pilots strike a relaxed pose in Campagne while being interrogated by the commander of I Gruppe, Hauptmann Hubertus von Bonin.

On 6 August 1940 fate finally caught up with the Kapitän of 1 Staffel during a dogfight. "Seppl" Seiler was photographed in the naval hospital at Hardinghem near Calais.

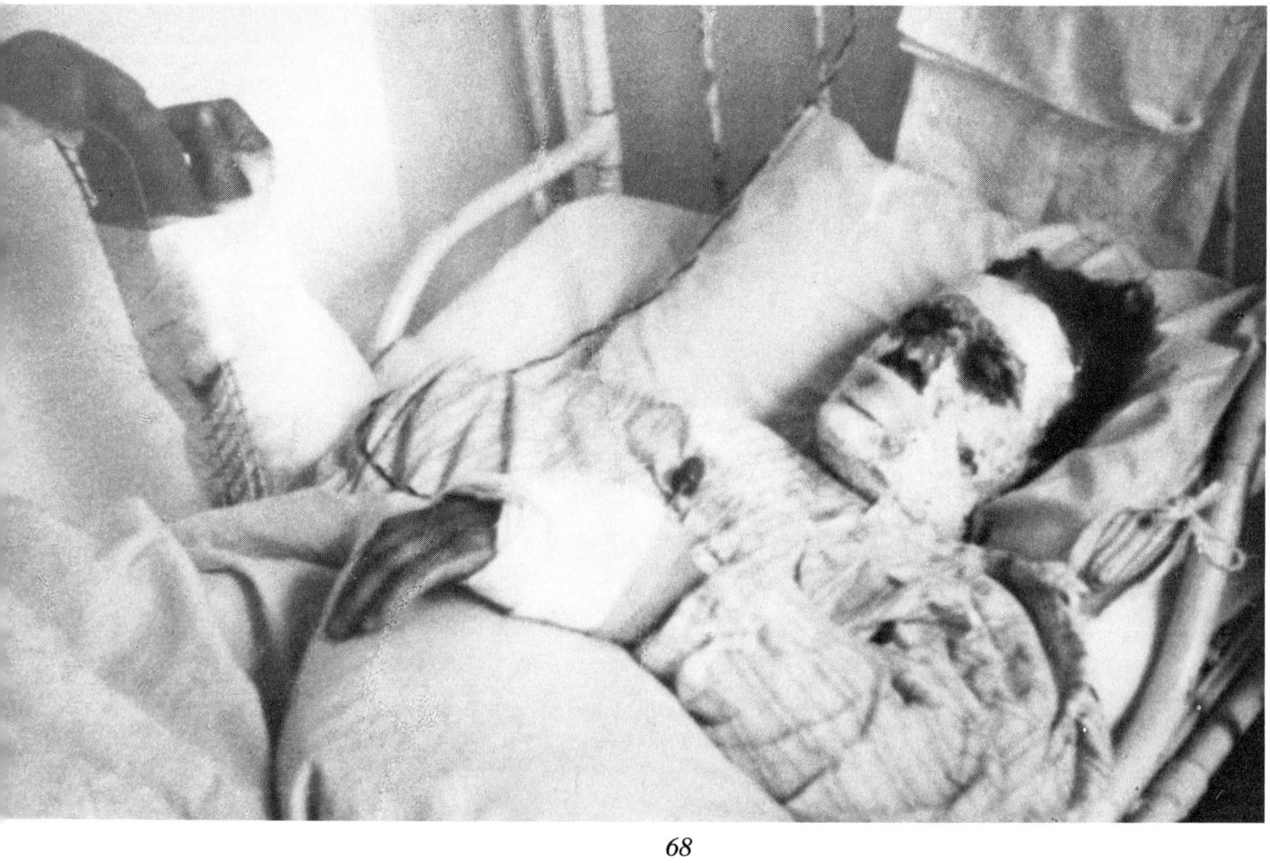

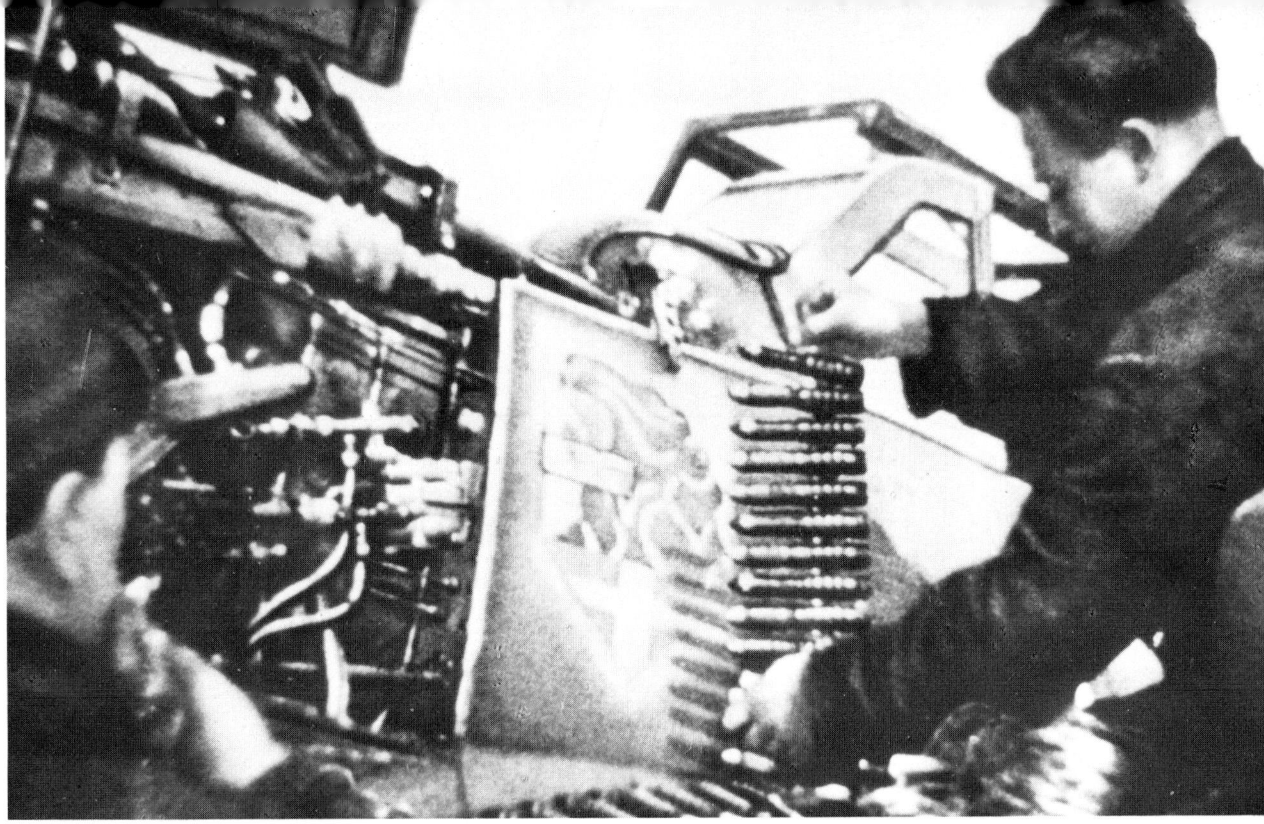

The "black men" have their hands full with things to do in order to get the fighters ready for combat again. With up to four missions per day, it was necessary to work 'round the clock. These are armorers of II Gruppe at work on an Bf 109E-4.

Pilots of III Gruppe: (from left) Leutnant Ostermann, Leutnant Fink, Leutnant Lange, Leutnant Wübke, Leutnant Hausmann, leutnant Zilken and Leutnant Bob during an afternoon on the town in Guines.

Although peeling potatoes isn't everyone's cup of tea, there will always be volunteers when it comes to satisfying one's appetite. Soldiers of 7 Staffel are seen here in a cooperative effort.

II Gruppe had by this time transferred from Harlinghem to Campagne as well. A Schwarm taxies from the dispersal area out to the takeoff point.

On 13 October 1940 the Kapitän of 4 Staffel, Oberleutnant Philipp, claimed his 16th, 17th, and 18th victories. Oberleutnant Pichon-Kalau von Hofe shares in the celebration, for he had scored his fourth kill the day before. Oberleutnant Philipp reached his 20th victory on 20 October, and on the 4th of November was the second pilot in the Geschwader to be awarded the Knight's Cross.

The Staffel emblems of 1, 2, and 3 Staffel and the symbol of the Stabskompanie, the "Schreckensteiner."

In September of 1940 a practical demonstration of one-man rubber life rafts was carried out. With stormy seas, climbing into them proved rather difficult, but in emergency situations the lifeboats proved themselves. The photo shows a critical jury. From left to right: Kommodore Major Trautloft, Oberst von Döring of Jafü 2, and Generaloberst Milch.

Air-sea rescue planes such as the He 59 patrolled the entire sea area of Luftflotte 2. These floatplanes were stationed in the harbor of Bolougne. Their operational area ranged from Dieppe to the German-Dutch coast. Many pilots who had either been shot down or forced to ditch owed their lives to the men of the Seenot-Staffel.

7 Staffel under the command of Oberleutnant Scholz was also based in Guines. After the Kommandeur of III Gruppe, Hauptmann Ultsch, was killed on 5 September, Oberleutnant Scholz led the unit for a brief period until Hauptmann Lignitz assumed command.

During the Battle of Britain the Teufelsstaffel (9 Staffel) flew from Guines and was the first Staffel of the Geschwader to conduct fighter-bomber missions against England.

Oberleutnant Bob bested his 19th opponent on 11 November 1940 and was awarded the Knight's Cross on 7 March 1941 for this feat.

Brothers-in-arms of II Gruppe in Guines. From left: Oberleutnant Zilken, Oberleutnant Bob and Feldwebel Pausinger.

Despite nonstop activity on the aircraft Werkmeister Feldwebel Ropperts and his maintenance crew of 1 Staffel have kept their sense of humor.

Armorers of 5 Staffel during sight alignment. 5 Staffel suffered a bitter loss on 20 November 1940 when Oberleutnant von Aspern fell in combat over England. He had brought down no less than 18 of the enemy in aerial combat.

Hauptfeldwebel Seliger, the Spiess of the Stabskompanie, seen here with a "live Schreckensteiner."

The air offensive against England had failed. Storms and rains prevented further large-scale operations, leaving only so-called "garbage missions" to be flown. The Gruppen of JG 54, along with the Gruppen of other Geschwader, were pulled back from the Channel and transferred to bases in the rear area.

II Gruppe took up winter R & R quarters at the airbase in Delmenhorst from 3 December 1940 to 23 January 1941. The photo shows officers bowling in Delmenhorst. From left: Graf Sponeck, Beisswenger, Philipp, ?, Pöhs, Marianka, Hein, and Mütherich in the foreground throwing the ball.

I Gruppe, by now blooded in combat, was transferred to Jever on 27 September 1940 and until May of 1941 was subordinated to Jagdgeschwader 1 for protection of the German Bight. For a short time, the Gruppe also provided detachments to the airbases at Wesermünde, Westerland, and Groningen in Holland. This is the dispersal area of 1 Staffel in Wesermünde.

Maintenance personnel of 1 Staffel during the crossing to Langeoog.

Oberleutnant Ködderitzsch, the Staffelkapitän of 1 Staffel in Westerland, March 1941. At the end of March Oberleutnant Ködderitzsch was the victim of a fatal crash while on a training flight in his Bf 109.

The period of winter peace naturally also provided a time for relaxation. Each member of the Geschwader was permitted to take well-deserved leave for a time. Pilots of the Geschwader spent a ski vacation together in Kitzbühel. In the clean, fresh air of the mountains the old vigor quickly returned. The photo was taken on the Hahnenkamm.

3 Staffel under Oberleutnant Schmoller-Haldy was based in Groningen/Elde in March of 1941. From here Leutnant Vinzent shot down a Spitfire. Still wearing his life vest, he reports to his Staffelkapitän (far right).

8 Staffel, under Oberleutnant Egger, was also based in Holland until its transfer to Dortmund.

Hauptmann von Bonin with officers of I/JG 54 in Wangerooge. There's gossip that the unit will soon be transferred again. From left to right: Oberleutnant Hein, Hauptmann von Bonin, Oberleutnant Graf von Matuschka, Oberleutnant Ludwig, and Leutnant Raub.

Geschwaderstab, II and II Gruppe deployed to France once again beginning on 15 January 1941. Flying from Le Mans and Cherbourg, the units provided air defense of Normandy for two months. Camouflage netting disguises a Stab aircraft in Le Mans.

Major Trautloft and Hauptmann Hrabak seem to have differing opinions. But: "only one of them is right." Waffenfeldwebel "Vati" Köhler keeps a discretely low profile in the background.

"Where's Kath?" It was possible that he could have become separated from the Schwarm or crash landed. Oberleutnant Kath eventually returned to base, overdue but unharmed. From right: Major Trautloft, Hauptmann der Reserve Waldhausen, Oberleutnant Pichon-Kalau von Hofe.

A game of rugby took place on 6 March 1941 during summertime temperatures in Le Mans between II Gruppe – beefed up by the Geschwaderstab – and III Gruppe. No one seemed to be bothered by the droning engines of the Ju 88 bombers taking off nearby.

Hauptmann Lignitz with officers of his III Gruppe during pistol firing practice. From right: Hauptmann Lignitz, Hausmann, Fink, Leykauf, and Schmidt (administration).

"Sonja" keeps watch on the "Emil." One of the numerous dogs of 8 Staffel in Le Mans.

Stab, II and III/JG 54 transferred to Austria by ground and air beginning on 29 March 1941 to take part in the campaign against Yugoslavia. The pilots flew their Messerschmitts southeast along the snow-capped alpine ranges . . .

. . . made an interim landing in Salzburg – here is an aircraft of 5 Staffel . . .

. . . and eventually arrived in Graz (II Gruppe) and Parendorf(III Gruppe), their planned airfields for initial operations.

The campaign in the Balkans against Yugoslavia began for the Grünherz fighters on 6 April and ended on 18 April 1941. The enemy only offered resistance in the air for the first three days – and the first aerial victories were scored. As the operation continued, attacks were directed against ground forces and supply routes of the enemy. Locomotives were the particular targets of the fighters, causing the fighting power of Yugoslavia to break up quite rapidly. For the first time, components of the ground personnel were called upon to demonstrate their effectiveness in an infantry role. The men were airlifted by four Ju 52 transports and – supported by strafing attacks from the pilots – captured the airfield at Bijeljina, holding it until German army troops arrived.

On April 18th the campaign ended, and units of the Geschwader gathered in Semlin, the large commercial airport of Belgrade. They waited there until new transfer orders arrived on 25 April, assigning the unit to Stolp-Reitz in Pomerania. The aircraft were transferred to Bucharest, where they were taken over by Jagdgeschwader 77 for continued operations against Greece and Crete. The ground personnel continued on via Klagenfurt to Pomerania, some travelling in their own vehicles and others proceeding by train. There the Geschwader, including I Gruppe, converted over to the new Bf 109F-2.

With 8 Staffel in Arad (Rumania). From left: Heinz Lange (wearing sunglasses), Paulisch, Heyer, Fischer, Pentenrieder.

Local ethnic Germans, or Volksdeutsche, tell their stories to the men of 5 Staffel in Bijeljina. The women have brought welcome gifts, such as milk and eggs.

The Semlin-Belgrade airport, last operational site of II Gruppe in this campaign. Note the undamaged aircraft hangars in the background.

In Semlin the elements of the Geschwader which had participated in the operation gathered together for reassignment to Stolp/Pomerania, travelling by road and rail to their new base.

On 12 May 1941 the bulk of the Geschwader arrived in Stolp.

The first days of June in Stolp. By this time the pilots had already been retrained on the factory-fresh Bf 109F-2. The last few days of peace are spent in these tent cities.

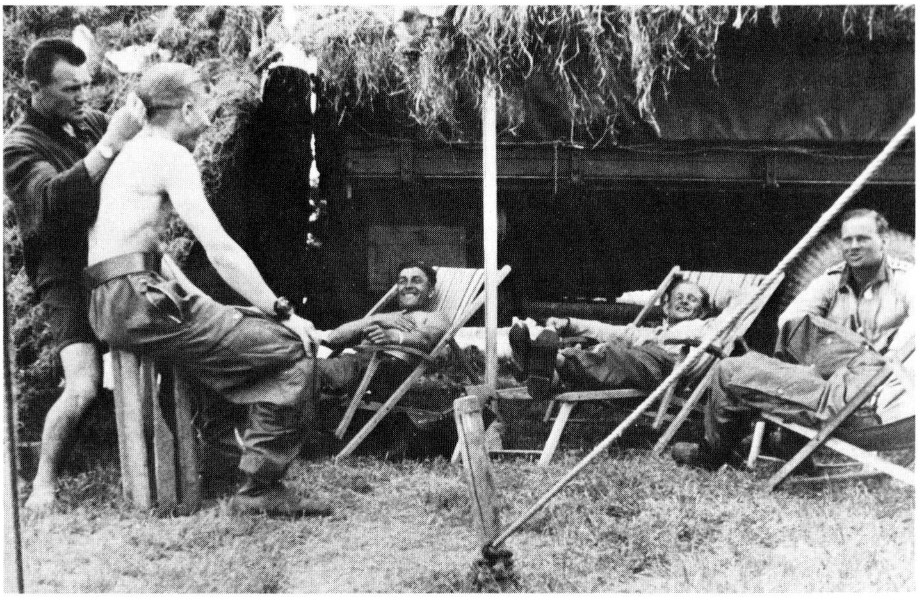

The barber of I Gruppe enjoys a brisk business at the airfield of Lindental in East Prussia. While Oberleutnant Ludwig, sitting on a wooden crate, is served, Unteroffizier Kittel, Oberleutnant Graf von Matuschka and Oberfeldwebel Fuchs wait in their comfortable lounge chairs until its their turn.

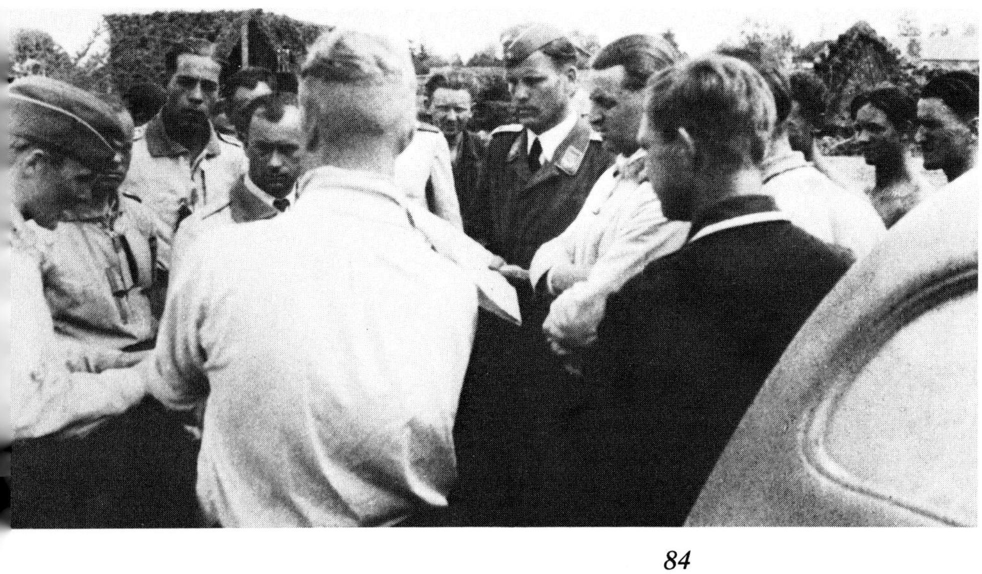

Final briefing between the commander, pilots and mechanics of I Gruppe. From left: Oberleutnant Götz, Oberleutnant Kinzinger, Hauptmann von Bonin, Oberwerkmeister Schröder, Waffenfeldwebel Höhle.

22 June 1941 – the Russian offensive begins. In the early morning hours the Gruppen of the Geschwader take off, strengthened by II/JG 53 under the command of Hauptmann Bretnütz – flying escort for the Kampfgeschwader of Luftflotte 1.

Counterattacks by the Russian air force – such as these SB-2 bombers under fire by German flak – were all beaten off with heavy losses suffered by the attackers.

During the first large-scale air battle over Dünaburg (Daugavpils) on 30 June 1941 the Geschwader succeeded in scoring 65 air victories. Scattered on the ground are the remains of Russian SB-2 bombers and the nimble Ratas.

While the pilots and key maintenance personnel jumped from one airfield to the next by air transport, the bulk of the ground crew made their tortured and tiresome way forward via jammed, miserable roads. This photo shows the transfer of 3 Staffel between Mitau and Jakobstadt (Jekabpils) at the end of June 1941.

The tent city at the Dünaburg airfield.

6 July 1941 – Dünaburg. The commander-in-chief of the 16th Armee, Generaloberst Busch, gives his thanks for the air protection provided to his forces. Left: Vice Gruppenkommandeur Oberleutnant Scholz. Center: Generaloberst Busch. Right: Major Trautloft.

Typical photos from the streets during the advance: shot up Russian tanks and other vehicles on the side of the road and in the fields. The heavy, ungainly looking KV-2 tank never failed to arouse the curiosity of the ground soldiers.

Understandably, there was particular interest in the enemy's fighters. This was particularly so for the two types which were most frequently encountered at the beginning of the campaign: the I-16 "Rata" and the I-153 (below). Hauptmann Hrabak and Oberleutnant "Fips" Philipp appraise a crash-landed I-16. On the left is Oberleutnant Schulz, the technical officer. "Minke-Pinke", Philipp's dachshund, is also naturally present.

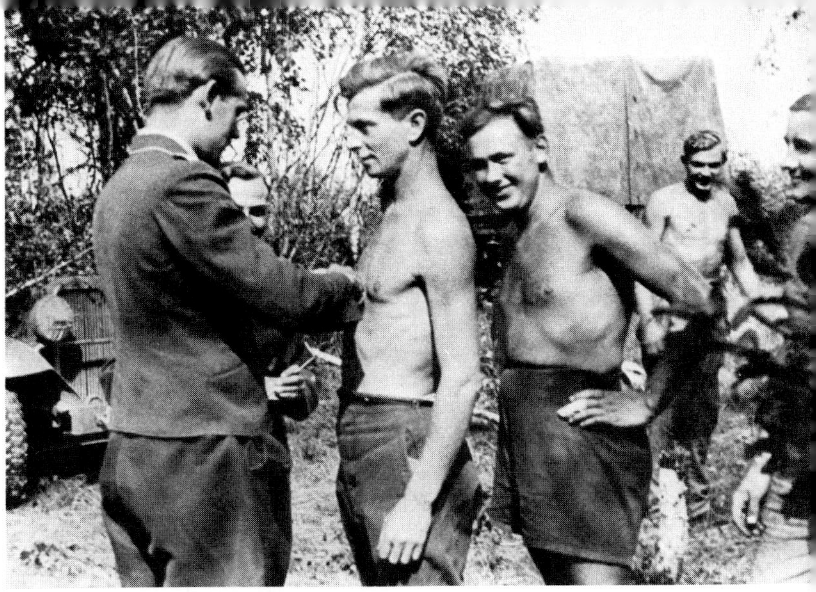

During the advance, Stabsarzt Dr. Thiemann administers typhoid shots.

A machine gun is fitted to all trucks for protection against surprise attacks. During the long journey the men of II Gruppe while away the time, each in his own way.

Each able-bodied man is needed whenever the vehicle becomes bogged down in mud or sand. During the trip from Ostrow to Sarudinje, every man is given the command "arms out and get to it!"

Oberst Werner Mölders and the Kommandeur of II Gruppe/JG 53, Hauptmann Bretnütz. This Gruppe was subordinated to JG 54 when Bretnütz was seriously injured during a mission on 22 June 1941. He died on 27 June in the hospital following the amputation of a leg.

Bf 109F-2s of II/JG 54 ready for takeoff, seen in front of a birch forest in Sarudinje. Summer 1941.

Post-mission briefing in Sarudinje. The Kommandeur of II Gruppe, Hauptmann Hrabak (left), with Oberleutnant Schulten (right) and Oberfeldwebel Max Stotz (center).

Hauptmann Hrabak and his Staffelkapitäne at the airfield of Samro Ozero. From left: Oberleutnant Philipp (4 Staffel), Kommandeur Hauptmann Hrabak, Oberleutnant Eckerle (6 Staffel), and Oberleutnant Mütherich (5 Staffel).

Their master's rapidly climbing tally of air victories seem of little interest to the two dachshunds of Oberleutnant Philipp, "Löwe" and "Minke-Pinke."

At the critical moment, the meticulous work of the armorers can decide victory or defeat.

July 1941 – Oberleutnant Schmoller-Haldy, Kapitän of 3 Staffel, gives his report to the Kommodore and his Gruppenkommandeur (I Gruppe), Hauptmann von Selle. The Kommodore had been wearing the Knight's Cross since 27 July 1941, which was presented to him after his 20th victory.

On 6 August 1941 the Kapitän of 5 Staffel, Oberleutnant "Hubs" Mütherich (with 31 victories), and Leutnant "Joschi" Pöhs, also of 5 Staffel (with 28 victories) were awarded the Knight's Cross in Samro Ozero. The Kommandeur and the Kapitän of 4 Staffel pose with the new recipients in a group photo. The happiness of the "black men" is quite apparent as well.

"Sewing hour" – a photo which speaks for itself.

Every opportunity is seized upon to make life on the front lines more endurable. The "black men" of I Gruppe during a community bath.

Supply vehicles of I Gruppe caught during a short break on the forest's edge. The opened doors, with 1 and 3 Staffel's coats-of-arms, provide a cooling draft.

The kitchen crew (II/JG 54) are always coming up with new ideas when it comes to providing variety in the menu. Whether it be a hearty noodle soup with chicken or a crispy schweinebraten, something can always be found. Even a hunt for hooded crow isn't just for sport.

The wild rabbits hunted back in Germany wouldn't taste any different than these four "munchers" brought in as proud trophies by Feldwebel Wefers and Unteroffizier Meissner.

Operationally, Jagdgeschwader 54 was subordinate to I Fliegerkorps under General der Flieger Förster (right), in the Luftflotte 1 district led by Generaloberst Keller (left).

September 1941 – Lissino airfield. Towing services to the runway across the softened taxiway is provided by a Maybach tractor.

The large number of enemy planes shot down are offset by the bitter losses on the part of the Geschwader. The young Leutnant Henkemeier from the Ergänzungsstaffel was shot down at the end of August over the island of Ösel. The remains of his machine were discovered after the island was taken.

Oberleutnant "Hubs" Mütherich, Staffelkapitän of 5 Staffel, met his death on 9 September 1941 when his Bf 109 flipped over during an emergency landing. Mütherich had a total of 43 air victories to his credit. Just in the East alone, 33 air duels were decided in his favor.

General Förster awards Hauptmann Franz Eckerle with the Knight's Cross on 18 September 1941 after his 30th victory. Eckerle was well known before the war as an aerobatic flyer.

"Fips" Philipp congratulates his radiant comrade. Hauptmann Eckerle assumed command of I Gruppe in December of 1941. on 14 February 1942 he was forced down by ground fire near Velikiye Luki and killed by Russian soldiers. Eckerle was posthumously honored with the award of the Oak Leaves.

In the summer of 1941 the Kommandeur of II Gruppe, Hauptmann Hrabak, awards outstanding members of the ground personnel with the War Service Cross (Kriegsverdienst-Kreuz).

Armorers – also known as "Waffenjodler" (lit. "weapons yodlers") – photographed during boresighting of the internal guns. Success hinged upon the scrupulous attention of the armorers and the flying abilities of the pilot.

Rotte by rotte, a Staffel taxis out for takeoff on yet another operational flight. The pilots are sure in the knowledge that they can count on the work of the "black men."

Reassignment once again. An advance team from II Gruppe on the arduous journey to a new airfield.

With just a few turns of the hand the personnel of the Geschwaderstab have created an open-air "dining hall."

This, too, is an important project: quick to set up (on the other side of camp, however), these were known as "Donnerbalken", or "thunder beams."

Among the great Experten of the Geschwader was Leutnant Max-Helmuth Ostermann. After the death of Mütherich he briefly led 5 Staffel. Then he was made Kapitän of 7 Staffel. On 4 September 1941 he was presented the Knight's Cross after 29 air victories. His fighter patrols took him deep into the Russian hinterland, where he would attack the enemy at his own airfields. The upper picture shows Ostermann in the center of his Staffel comrades.

Lower photo: Leutnant Ostermann preparing to take off. His rudder tally shows 33 kills.

Hauptmann Wandel (center), Gruppenadjutant of II Gruppe and later Kapitän of 5 Staffel, in Rjelbitzi. On the left (with pipe) is Leutnant Kretschmer.

In the fall of 1941 the Gruppen of the Geschwader occupied the well-built (by Russian standards) airbases of Siverskaya and Krasnogvardeysk as well as the airfields at Rjelbitzi and Staraya Russa. The aerial photo shows the Shelon River, with the Rjelbitzi airfield on the left.

In Krasnogvardeysk – also called Gatschina – Stuka and bomber units also resided for a time. Several wings of the Gatschina palace, once the summer residence of the Russian czars, were still in such good condition that the occupied rooms soon became quite hospitable.

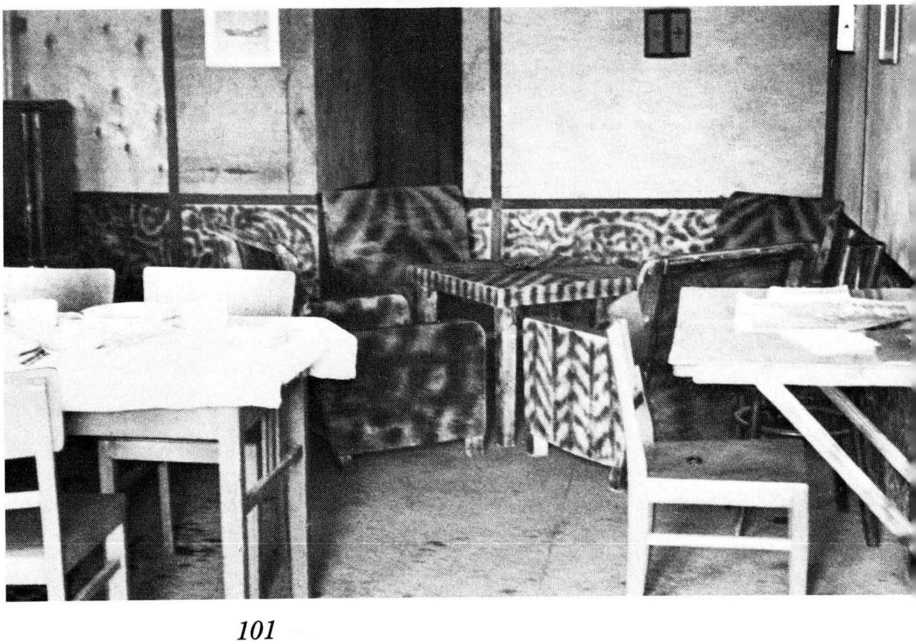

Recreation and dining room for the pilots in Gatschina.

1 Staffel has set up home here: the banner with the chimney sweep and names of former operational sites flutters in the autumn breeze. The Kapitän of 1 Staffel, Hauptmann Seiler, assumed command of III Gruppe after Hauptmann Lignitz was shot down over Leningrad on 30 September. Oberleutnant Heinz Lange was then put in command of the Staffel.

Russian bombers and attack aircraft repeatedly tried to attack German occupied airfields. The heavily armored IL-2 "Stormoviks", in particular, paid a high price for their surprise attacks.

The successful returning flyers of I Gruppe were welcomed home to Krasnogvardeysk by a victory bell and a shot fired from "loud Eberhard."

The unannounced Russian winter of 1941/1942 presented unknown, serious problems to the "black men." More primitive aids – often learned from prisoners – were employed. Even a pony-drawn panje cart is more suited to delivering fuel to the parked aircraft than tank trucks, which would often get stuck in the soft earth.

Even the village street in Rjelbitzi has turned into a mud track.

A discussion among the maintenance crew and the pilot. The Russian winter brings with it new problems for everyone. Feldwebel Heinz Schmitz, Oberwerkmeister Fritz Treiber, and Waffenwart August Wagner of 3 Staffel.

Photograph of a wingman taken during a combat flight by 4 Staffel over the vast Russian landscape.

A Rotte ready for the next mission. In the foreground are 500 kg Stuka bombs of the "Immelmänner" (Stuka-Geschwader Immelmann).

The signposts pointing the way to Jagdgeschwader "Trautloft"'s command post (Gefechtsstand) could be found everywhere at road junctions in the northern sector of the Eastern Front.

The entrance to the Geschwader command post in Siverskaya could not be missed, due to the two bears standing in front of it. An ideal backdrop for group photos. The NCOs of the Geschwaderstab are (from left to right): Unteroffizier Gruber, Feldwebel Riechers, Unteroffizier Preger, Unteroffizier Schmidt, Feldwebel Dubiella, Unteroffizier Kastenholz, Unteroffizier Domschke, ?, Unteroffizier Bolsum, and Feldwebel Echterling.

The Kommodore's airplane seen during maintenance.

A good photo of a Messerschmitt fighter which has just landed.

Rjelbitzi – for reasons of camouflage the warming tent and vehicles are covered with white tarpaulins. The aircraft parked in the foreground are being fueled and serviced.

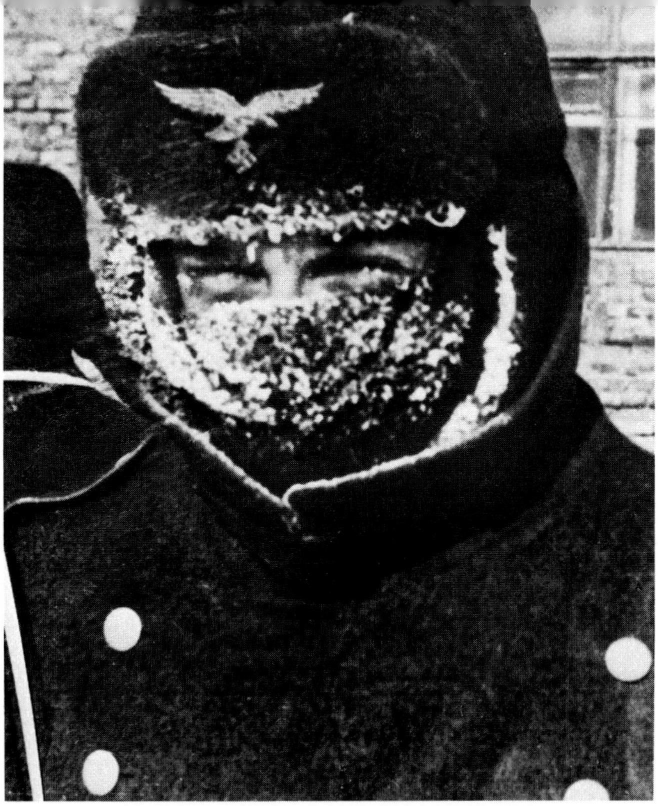

The first Russian winter caught the German units unprepared. It naturally hit the infantry in the trenches and foxholes particularly hard. But even the men working on the fighters, who worked with tools of iron in temperatures of -40 degrees Celsius, had to give superhuman effort. The enemy, who was used to the cold, incessantly attacked German positions. The Luftwaffe then was called upon to jump in and help.

These two pictures – showing man and beast – give some feeling for the icy cold of the 1941/42 winter.

Pilots also had to suffer with the cold. The Staffelkapitän's "vehicle" (here a sleigh) of 9 Staffel, was driven by two reliable "horsepower." Oberleutnant Bob and Hein Wübke have quickly learned how to drive the Russian ponies in Siverskaya.

Even at 42 degrees below the aircraft must be kept ready for combat. The aircraft of Oberleutnant Bob is seen during pre-warming. The bomb racks can be clearly seen below the slender fuselage.

Leutnant Horst Ademeit and Leutnant Ostermann in winter "packing" in Siverskaya.

Four successful pilots of the Geschwader, who despite the biting cold haven't lost their sense of humor. From left to right: Bob, Wübke, Eisenach and Fink.

Men of the Gruppenflakzug (Gruppe AA platoon) behind a 20mm AA gun fending off an attacking Soviet IL-2.

This picture was taken a few months later. The damage caused by Russian attack planes can be seen (Siverskaya).

The men of the Fernsprechzug (communications platoon, here of II Gruppe) played an important role in the operation of a Geschwader. In any weather, whether rain or snow, a troop had to be prepared to find and repair damaged lines. Photo: Unteroffizier Eisele and Obergefreiter Vogel during line setup in Rjelbitzi.

Obergefreiter Moser from the Fernsprechzug of II Gruppe at the "voicebox" in Siverskaya. 120 connections could be made from here.

Feldwebel Tegtmeier (left) and Unteroffizier Bremer (right), two old Staffel friends from 2 Staffel. Fritz Tegtmeier became Kapitän of 3 Staffel in August of 1944 after he was presented the Knight's Cross on 28 March 1944 following 99 air victories. Peter Bremer was made a POW in Russia. On 13 July he had to bale out near Orel after being hit by flak, eventually returning home after six long years of imprisonment.

Christmas 1941: the Kommodore, now promoted to Oberstleutnant, as guest of 9 Staffel. Next to him on his left is the acting Kapitän of 9 Staffel, Oberleutnant Zilken.

Oberstleutnant Günther Lützow, Kommodore of Jagdgeschwader 3 "Udet" and friend of Hannes Trautloft, pays a visit to the Grünherzgeschwader in Siverskaya. Here, too, the command post entrance serves as a backdrop for a scrapbook photo.

The Kommodore with officers of the Geschwaderstab. From left: H. Böttcher, O. Kath, Kommodore, R. Fikenscher, N. von Stelzer, S. Reymann.

Aside from a sauna during the winter there was also an airbase cinema in Siverskaya. Both establishments were well frequented.

Hauptmann Sattig (left, in flying helmet) was a recon pilot before cross-training to fighters in 1941. With II Gruppe, he eventually commanded 6 Staffel. He scored 53 air victories in the East until being reported as missing in action after being shot down on 10 August 1942 near Rzhev. On the right is Leutnant Beisswenger, who then took over the Staffel.

Gefreiter "Quax" Schnörrer (left) after his first kill on 31 December 1941. Lt. Ademeit, his Schwarmführer in 1 Staffel, reports to the Kapitän of 1 Staffel, Oblt. Heinz Lange (center).

Each one tried to shorten the long winter evenings in his own way. Inspektor Schmidt (standing) and Hauptmann Hrabak follow an intense game of chess between Gruppenarzt Dr. Kettner and an Oberleutnant of II Gruppe.

The Rotte of Spanke/ Bremer on a free ranging fighter sweep over the Volkhov front. The airplanes still wear the winter camouflage pattern.

View from a Fieseler Storch to the runway of the airfield at Rjelbitzi.

Field training – a non-commissioned officer's training course is conducted on the wide field at the Siverskaya airbase.

Leutnant Horst Hannig, a pilot with 5 Staffel, converses with Gruppenadjutant Wandel. Wandel was made Kapitän of 5 Staffel in May of 1942.

On 14 February 1942 the Kommandeur of I Gruppe, Hauptmann Eckerle, fell in combat. His successor was Hauptmann Philipp. Command of 4 Staffel was assumed by Oberleutnant Wengel.

Oberst Adolf Galland, who was named General der Jagdflieger following the death of Werner Mölders, paid a visit to the Geschwader units fighting on the Eastern Front in March of 1942. In Rjelbitzi the Kommodore of the Grünherzgeschwader greets his guest. The group photo shows from left to right: Hauptmann Wandel, Hauptmann Brustellin, Oberst Galland, Hauptmann Hrabak, Oberstleutnant Trautloft, Oberleutnant Späte, Major Janke, and Leutnant Hannig.

The country is still buried in snow, but the sun's rays are beginning to gain strength. In "Ringelpietz" (the German nickname for Rjelbitzi) Professor Otto Haase, Hauptmann Hrabak, the Kommodore, and Oberleutnant Schulten (from left to right) enjoy the warm sunshine.

The armorers and mechanics of 5 Staffel are also glad that the long winter is finally over.

The "snow-ski days" for the modified Klemms (Kl 35) are numbered. The wing of one of the planes also serves as an ideal spot for a noontime siesta.

NCOs of 2 Staffel in the dining hall at Gatschina – spring of 1942. Of the seven pilots shown here, five were later awarded the Knight's Cross (Ritterkreuz, or RK). From left to right: Ofw. Wöhnert (RK 6 December 1944), Fw. Fuchs, Fw. Tegtmeier (RK 28 March 1944), Uffz. Kroschinski (RK 17 April 1945), Fw. Broennle (RK 14 March 1943), Uffz. Grollmus (RK 6 October 1944, posthumously), and Uffz. Koch.

Oberfeldwebel Rudolf Klemm is credited with making the Geschwader's 2000th victory on 4 April 1942. This group photo was taken in front of the scoring aircraft (from 8 Staffel): left is Oberleutnant Fink, then Oberfeldwebel Klemm and Hauptmann Jung.

Leutnant Erwin Leykauf was shot down 25 kilometers behind Russian lines. In an adventuresome fashion he succeeded in returning to his own lines. In the center is Leutnant Leykauf; to his right, half-hidden, is the Kommandeur of III Gruppe, Hauptmann Seiler.

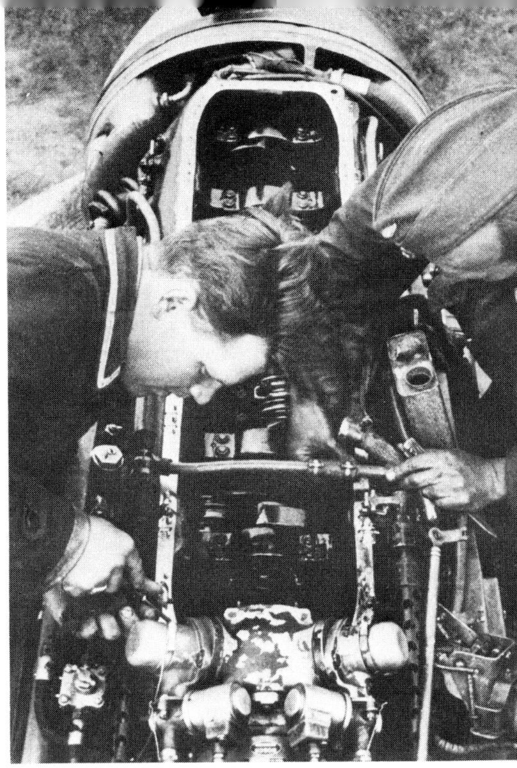

View from above showing the 12-cylinder Daimler-Benz DB 601 engine of an Bf 109 – the daily workplace for the engine mechanics.

A pastoral morning scene at an airfield of II Gruppe. The pilots stand shivering in the buffalo grass, awaiting their orders to fly.

Escort for Ju 52 transports bringing supplies into the Dem'yansk pocket. "White 6" of 7 Staffel is wingtip to wingtip with a Junkers transport.

A photo of their protective charges – the performance of the German transport units during the Second World War was extraordinary. It should be remembered here the heavy losses suffered by the supply flights into the pocket at Stalingrad.

A fighter sweep over Volkhov; Oberleutnant Pichon-Kalau von Hofe with his Schwarm.

On 9 May 1942 General Förster presented the Knight's Cross to Leutnant Hans Beisswenger and Leutnant Horst Hannig, both of 6 Staffel. Kommodore Trautloft and the Kommandeur of II Gruppe, Hrabak, pose for the photographer with the newest RK recipients. In the center is General Förster.

Lower photo: a snapshot taken in front of the Gruppe command post in Rjelbitzi.

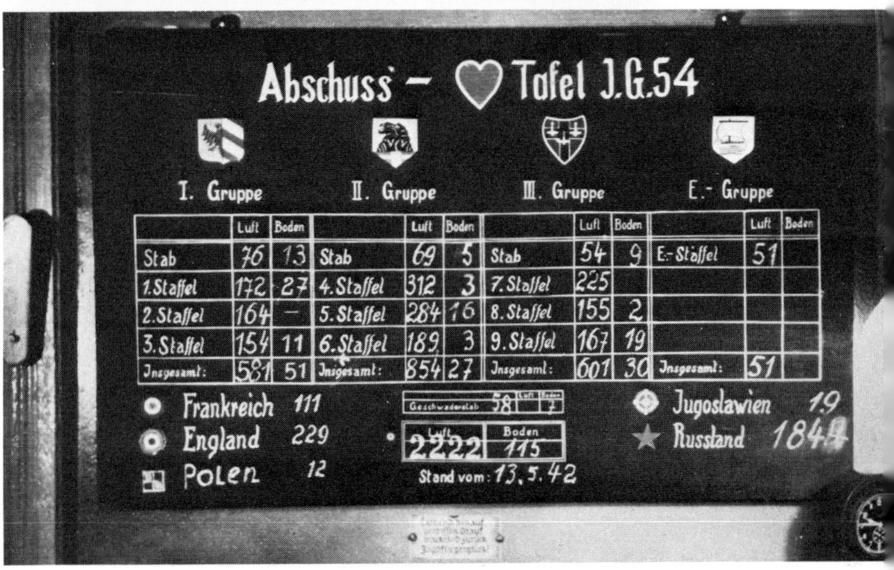

The scoreboard of Jagdgeschwader 54 on 13 May 1942.

Upper left: An Bf 109 drifts in for a landing with its landing flaps extended.

Upper right: Oberfeldwebel Wilhelm Schilling returns from the 500th combat sortie flown by the "Teufelsstaffel" (9 Staffel), joyfully greeted by one of the Staffel dogs. Left: Leutnant Frenzel-Beyme; right: Oberwerkmeister Hölzner.

Left: The Kommandeur of III Gruppe, "Seppl" Seiler during a "welcome drink." From left to right: Hauptmann Seiler, Staffelkapitän Bob, Frenzel-Beyme, Kromer, Schilling, Zweigert, and Müller (half-hidden).

Looking self-assured and proud, the "Grünherz-Dackel" of the Kommodore poses for the camera.

Two later Knight's Cross recipients – seen here at the beginning of their fighter careers. Above: Unteroffizier Rudi Rademacher returning from a successful mission. Below: Unteroffizier Karl Schnörrer with his aircraft mechanics.

Two of the armorers of 4 Staffel seen on the job – Karl Göcker and Leo Hengesbach.

4 Staffel preparing for a fighter-bomber mission.

Mechanics of the Geschwaderstab at work on "their" plane.

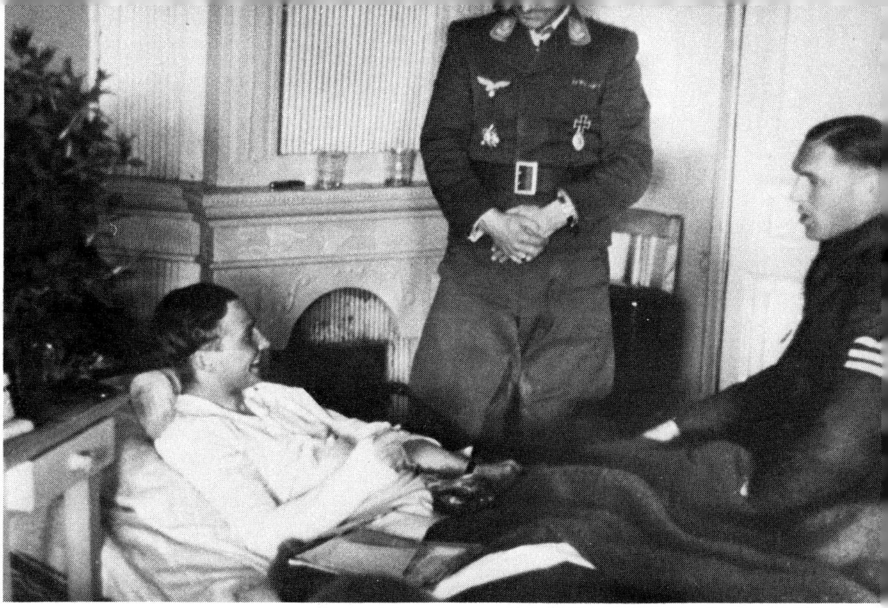

Oberleutnant Ostermann was wounded while scoring his 100th kill. Despite this, he was still able to bring his plane in for a smooth landing at Lyuban, just behind the front lines. The Kommodore and the Gruppenkommandeur visit with the cheerful patient in the hospital in Siverskaya (June 1942). While still in the hospital, Ostermann was awarded the "Swords."

20 mm quad-mounted AA gun of the Flakzug from I Gruppe in Vyazma-Gradina.

An IL-2 shot down over Vyazma-Gradina.

During the Volkhov battle (13 January 1942 to 27 July 1942) the pilots of the Grünherz-geschwader flew night missions in the East for the first time with the Bf 109. Every German soldier on the Eastern Front has unpleasant memories of the Russian air force's activities during the night hours. The Grünherz fighters brought down 56 enemy aircraft over the Volkhov pocket without suffering a single loss to themselves. Hauptmann Seiler stood at the peak of the four most successful "night fighters" with 16 night kills, followed by Oberleutnant Fink with 9 and Leutnant Leykauf with 8 kills. Finally, Leutnant Heyer scored 6 nighttime kills over the Volkhov battlefield.

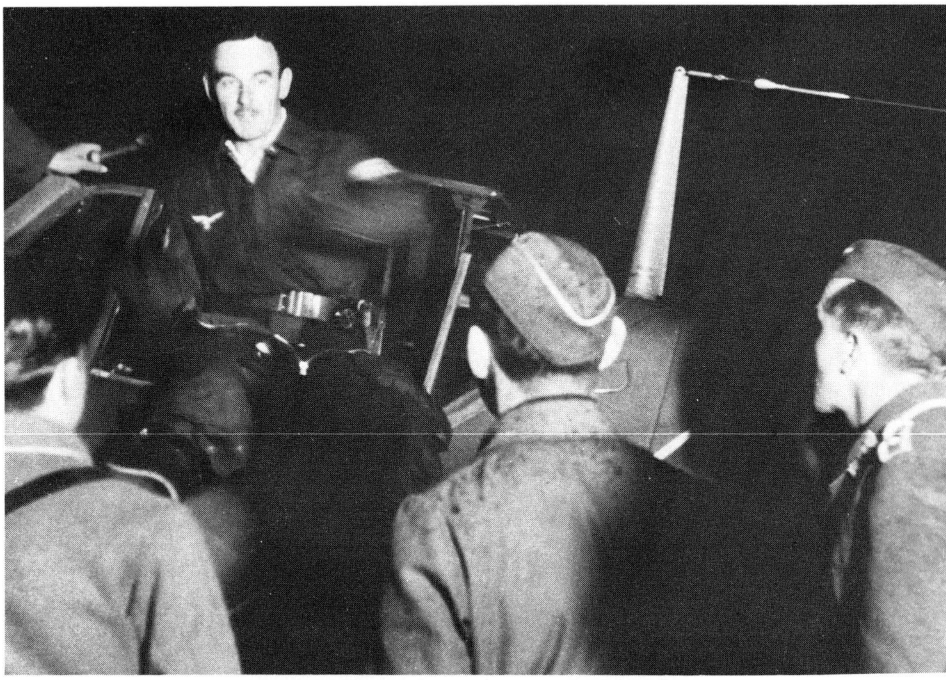

Oberleutnant Fink seen upon returning from a successful night sortie.

Among Leutnant Heyer's (center) 53 victories there were 6 night kills. Heyer collided with a Russian fighter over Leningrad on 9 November 1942 and crashed. He was listed as missing in action.

Generaloberst Keller presents a silver goblet to Leutnant Leykauf for exceptional performance during night operations. In the night of 22-23 June 1942 he shot down a total of six enemy aircraft and in doing so raised his victory tally to 23. Photo center: Hauptmann Seiler.

In July of 1942 Feldwebel Otto Kittel was married "long-distance" in Krasnogvardeysk. Per regulation, he appears before his Kommandeur, Hauptmann Philipp (who performed the wedding), wearing his steel helmet and service uniform.

This group photograph of 3 Staffel pilots was taken during the summer of 1942 in Krasnogvardeysk. From left to right: Kulga, Diepgen, Brand, Forbrig, Rademacher, Guth, Siegler (RK posthumously), Tietze, Beutin, Lanzenbacher, Krutzke, Oberleutnant Götzke, Leutnant Fischer (both standing above right).

The Kommodore of the Grünherz fighters, Oberstleutnant Trautloft, and his three Gruppenkommandeure. From left to right: Hauptmann Seiler (III Gruppe), Hauptmann Hrabak (II Gruppe), the Kommodore, and Hauptmann Philipp (I Gruppe).

Again and again, the airfields come under fire from Russian artillery and aerial attacks. Here, the airplane of 1 Staffel's Kapitän, Oberleutnant Lange, has been severely damaged in Krasnogvardeysk by artillery fire.

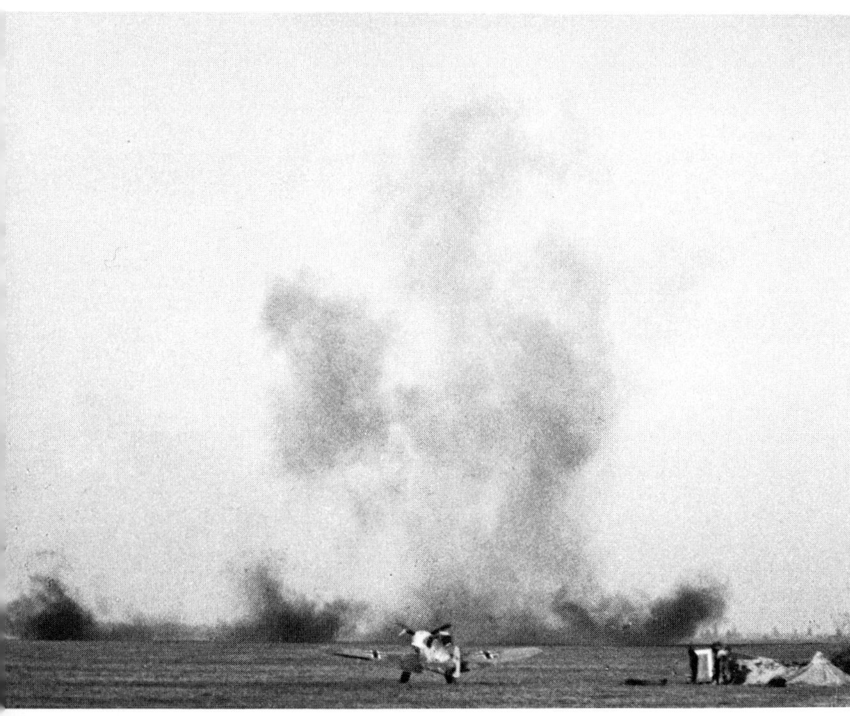

This is what it looked like at the airfield in Siverskaya following a bombing raid.

During the humid summer days, mosquitoes came up in droves from the swamps and made life miserable. Only by donning mosquito netting could the "black men" carry out their work on the airplanes.

Leutnant Kretschmer also tried to keep away the pesky torturers with a smoking pipe, while the Kapitän of 5 Staffel, Hauptmann Wandel, has apparently been using a cream.

With helmet, leash and carbine, the "prisoners" are herded toward the kitchen.

Under the protection of an anti-aircraft machine gun . . .

. . . everyone uses his free time to enjoy his hobby. Feldwebel Stöber, along with others from 7 Staffel, has set up a vegetable garden in Siverskaya. Under the protecting cover of shrubbery, young plants are growing in the wooden frame.

Hauptmann Hrabak and the "Professor", Otto Haase, have plans for a refreshing bath.

The pilots of 5 Staffel with their Kapitän, Hptm. "Gnom" Wandel (center). Lt. Horst Hannig (left) and Lt. Wolfgang Kretschmer (right). Hptm. Wandel fell in combat with Russian fighters on 7 October 1942 southeast of Lake Ilmen after achieving 75 air victories. The Staffel was then temporarily led by Lt. Hannig.

Just as successful, 6 Staffel was led by Hauptmann Sattig. From left to right: Unteroffizier Fieber, Feldwebel Schleinhege, Feldwebel Büchner, Unteroffizier Wolff, Unteroffizier Nickel, Hauptmann Sattig, Unteroffizier Klopp, Leutnant Beisswenger, Unteroffizier Runge, and Unteroffizier Wernicke. Hauptmann Sattig (53 kills, RK posthumously) was listed as missing following a dogfight, and the Staffel was then taken over by Leutnant Beisswenger.

The world ski champion of 1941, Unteroffizier Toni Pfeifer (right) during a game of table tennis with Leutnant Waller. Unteroffizier Pfeifer fell in combat on 6 October 1942.

The Nachrichtenkompanie has set up their radio equipment in an abandoned Russian farmhouse in Rjelbitzi.

The men of the Nachrichtenkompanie also lived in the typical Russian peasant houses. The tile stove radiates comforting warmth, so that one's free time is spent in the large living room along with duty time. In the center of his colleagues sits Unteroffizier Georg Leber, who would later become the Federal German Defense Minister.

Oberfeldwebel Wilhelm Schilling was seriously injured by flak in the late fall on a combat flight. Oberleutnant Bob, Staffelkapitän of 9 Staffel, presents the courageous pilot with the Knight's Cross on 10 October 1942 in the hospital in Siverskaya.

The Geschwader's aircraft inventory also included a Fieseler "Storch", the Fi 156. In winter the wheels were replaced by snow skis. Due to the extremely short landing and takeoff distance, the "Storch" could be flown virtually anywhere and was therefore "everyone's girl."

The Kapitän of 6 Staffel, Oberleutnant Beisswenger, is seen travelling by horse sleigh in Rjelbitzi. Beisswenger had been awarded the Oak Leaves on 30 September 1942 after his 100th kill.

Leutnant Friedrich Rupp, a pilot from 7 Staffel, brought down his 50th enemy plane on 30 December 1942. His colleagues welcomed the successful pilot back to Velikiye Luki with an enlarged version of the Knight's Cross.

Major "Assi" Hahn led II Gruppe from 1 November 1942 on. His predecessor, Major Hrabak, took over Jagdgeschwader 52 as its Kommodore. "Assi" Hahn came from Jagdgeschwader 2 "Richthofen" and was one of the most successful pilots on the Western Front over the Channel. On 26 January 1943 Hahn landed in Staraya Russa after scoring his 100th victory.

That evening in Rjelbitzi, three successful Jagdflieger from the Geschwader met to celebrate the 100th by "Assi" Hahn (left) and the 150th kill by Leutnant Max Stotz (center). Oberleutnant Beisswenger is the third in the group; he had passed his 100th victory a long time previously. Major Hahn was listed as missing in action on 21 February 1943 after a dogfight over the "throat" of Dem'yansk. He eventually returned to his homeland after seven years as a POW. His successor in the leadership of II Gruppe was Hauptmann Jung, whose Staffel was taken over by Oberleutnant Graf von Matuschka.

Oberleutnant Graf von Matuschka, formerly Kapitän of 2 Staffel, now led 4 Staffel.

In February of 1943 pilots of I Gruppe were retrained on the Focke-Wulf Fw 190 by Staffel in Heiligenbeil. The robust airplane was more suited for fighter combat and low-level attacks in the East.

In Krasnogvardeysk, the dispersal area of I Gruppe, the "new bird" also quickly found favor in the eyes of the "black men."

Particularly apparent here is the difference between the Bf 109 and the Fw 190. The robust BMW 801 radial engine, with a performance of 1700 hp, gave the pilot a sense of security – by its looks alone. The wide track landing gear as well – unlike the Bf 109 – made landings a piece of cake.

"White 9" with "Quax" Schnörrer at the controls, photographed during an escort mission over the never-ending Russian landscape.

Snow is kicked up into swirling clouds as the heavy Fw 190 reaches land speeds of 180 kmh.

Feldwebel Otto Kittel scored the 4000th kill for the Grünherzgeschwader on 19 February 1943. This number is of particular significance when one is reminded that 4 April 1942 was the date of the 2000th victory. Which means that in ten months 2000 enemy aircraft were brought down.

In both pictures the guest of honor, Feldwebel Kittel, sits next to the Kommodore on his left.

Just one month later Fw. Kittel was reported missing in action following a combat mission. On 15 March he was forced to make a crash landing behind Russian lines after his airplane took crippling hits. Three days later he reported in to his Gruppe from the frontmost German lines. Kittel is given a welcome greeting in Staraya-Russa by Oblt. Götz (right) and Ofw. Broennle (left). The effects of his ordeal are still quite evident from his face.

Oberleutnant Edwin Dutel, Gruppenadjutant under Hauptmann Philipp, was the leader of a special fighter-bomber (Jabo) unit. Dutel was considered the "Jabo King" of JG 54. Primarily operating in the northern sector of the Eastern Front, his targets were supply and transportation convoys, transport ships on Lake Ladoga, tank concentrations and enemy positions. Oberleutnant Dutel fell 24 kilometers southeast of Schlüsselburg on a fighter-bomber mission.

During the winter of 1942/1943 a conference was held with the General der Flieger, during which it was determined that JG 26 would be rotated with JG 54 (Western-Eastern Front). I/JG 26 under Major Johannes Seifert, beefed up by 7 Staffel with Oberleutnant Mietusch, arrived in the East at the beginning of February 1943. III/JG 54 under Major "Seppl" Seiler and 4 Staffel under Oberleutnant Graf von Matuschka transferred to Vendeville near. Lille. This photo shows Oberleutnant Mietusch (far left) next to Hauptmann Philipp, Hauptmann Kelch and Oberleutnant Götz.

Oberleutnant Gerhard Koall (third from left) led 3 Staffel from March 1942.

At the end of March 1943 Oberst Trautloft bid adieu to the successful and beloved Kommandeur of I Gruppe, Major Hans Philipp, who from 1 April was to become the Kommodore of Jagdgeschwader 1 fighting in the West.

The Gruppe is formed up into an open square – here, 3 Staffel.

Good-byes from the officers of the Gruppe. From right: Oberleutnant Fischer, Oberleutnant "Bazi" Weiss, Oberleutnant Vinzent.

Oberleutnant Walter Nowotny, Kapitän of 1 Staffel since 25 October 1943, returns to Nikolskoye on 15 June 1943 after his 100th victory. Oberleutnant Eisenach (right), since May 1943 Kapitän of 3 Staffel, congratulates him.

Heino Cordes and "Quax" Schnörrer, two friends always ready for a prank.

The three successful pilots of the famous Nowotny Schwarm. From left to right: Oberfeldwebel Anton Döbele (RK 26 March 1944 posthumous), Unteroffizier Karl Schnörrer (RK 22 March 1945), and Oberfeldwebel Rudolf Rademacher (RK 30 September 1944). Combined, these three men accounted for no less than 266 of the enemy.

Oberst Trautloft was appointed on 5 July 1943 to a posting in the Stab (Headquarters) of the General der Jagdflieger as "Inspizient (Inspector) der Jagdflieger Ost." The new Geschwaderkommodore was Major Hubertus von Bonin (center). The Kommodore is seen in discussion with Oberleutnant Nowotny (left) and Leutnant Gerhard Loos, who in September would take over command of 8 Staffel in the West.

Oberfeldwebel Heinrich Sterr (left) and Unteroffizier Albin Wolf in August 1943 in Orel. Both were quite successful with 6 Staffel. At the time of the photo, Sterr had just scored his 50th air victory. His Knight's Cross was presented after his 86th kill. He fell on 26 November 1944 as a Staffelkapitän in IV Gruppe during the defense of the Reich. Wolf received the Knight's Cross after 117 victories. On 2 April 1944 he was fatally injured by Russian flak and posthumously awarded the Oak Leaves for his 144 victories.

The Flakzug of II Gruppe has been quite successful in fending off Russian attack planes. This 20 mm AA gun carries eleven confirmed kill rings on its barrel.

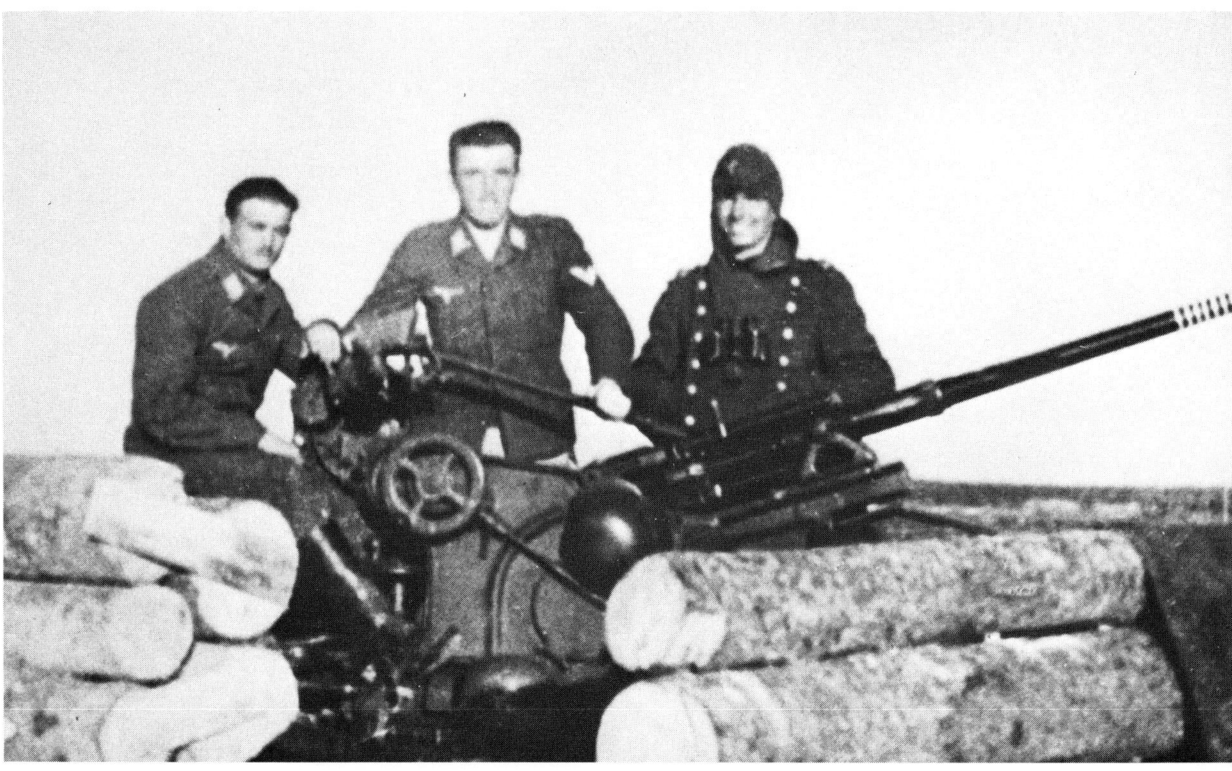

A Rotte of I Gruppe conducting a free-ranging fighter sweep in the area of Vyazma -Orel. The Fw 190 is quite popular with the pilots – and feared by the enemy.

Leutnant Günther Scheel developed into a successful fighter pilot in a very short period of time. Although he only arrived in Russia with 3 Staffel in the spring of 1943, by July of that year he had bested 71 of the enemy. On 16 July 1943 he rammed into an enemy plane and fell to his death. He was posthumously awarded the Knight's Cross on 5 December 1943.

Leutnant Karl Kempf, a pilot in III Gruppe, remains unforgotten in the annals of the Geschwader. He was presented the Knight's Cross as an Oberfeldwebel on 4 February 1942 after 41 victories. While flying with 2 Staffel of JG 26 in the West, Kempf was jumped by Mustangs during takeoff on 3 September 1944 and shot down. His final score stood at 65 kills.

General der Flieger Ritter von Greim (left) lands with a "Storch" at an airfield in the Orel operations area to be briefed on the situation in the air. "Operation Zitadelle", the last German offensive in the East, couldn't provide the German units with the change of fortune they needed.

The Kommodore, Major von Bonin, and Nachrichtenoffizier Oberleutnant Peter Lock (center) accept the post-flight reports of two pilots. Shatalovka, July 1943.

Oberleutnant Nowotny (second from left) was credited with a total of 49 aerial victories in August of 1943 alone. His 150th opponent fell on 18 August and twenty days later the "magic 200" was passed. In the photo to the left of Nowotny is Oberleutnant Vinzent.

Oberleutnant Max Stotz, wearer of the Oak Leaves and Kapitän of 5 Staffel, was one of the Experten of the Geschwader. He enjoyed his final string of victories during the early summer months of 1943. On 19 August 1943 Stotz's plane was hit by Russian fighters over enemy territory near Vitebsk and he was forced to bail out. He was declared missing in action. Oberleutnant Stotz was victorious a total of 189 times in combat.

The successes achieved by Walter Nowotny, promoted to Hauptmann on 1 October, never broke off. On 14 October the 250th enemy fell victim to his guns. With this, the 22-year old Hauptmann was at the pinnacle of all German fighter pilots.

Oberfeldwebel Otto Kittel was awarded the Knight's Cross on 29 October 1943 by Oberst Reuss. Major von Bonin was among the first to congratulate him and adjusts the Knight's Cross in "better light."

Hauptmann Nowotny also came in the "Weihe" (Fw 58) to the awards ceremony.

After "Seppl" Seiler was wounded (last posting as Kommandeur of I Gruppe) Hauptmann Nowotny was assigned command of the Gruppe. The photo shows Oberst Reuss (center) in conversation with Hauptmann Nowotny and Oberfeldwebel Kittel.

He, too, has crossed the "magic 100." Smiling, Oberfeldwebel Albin Wolf climbs down from his Focke-Wulf. On 22 November 1943 Wolf was awarded the Knight's Cross. By then his tally stood at 117.

The third Russian winter shows its claws yet again. This "pilot's memorial" occurred on an iced-over taxiway.

Toni Döbele, a born Swabian, flew in the famous Nowotny Schwarm. He scored 94 victories in 458 combat missions. On 26 March 1944 he was posthumously awarded the Knight's Cross.

Leutnant Anton Döbele collided in the air with another German fighter pilot just over the taxiway at Smolensk-Vitebsk and fell to his death. His comrades pay their last respects to him in an aircraft hangar. On the left is Oberleutnant Kittel; behind him is Oberfeldwebel Rademacher. Right front: Oberfeldwebel Wöhnert, and behind him, Oberfeldwebel Tegtmeier. The Kommandeur of I Gruppe, Hauptmann Nowotny, gives the eulogy and offers his last farewell to his friend.

This photo was taken in December 1943 in Orsha. From left: Oberleutnant Lützen, Oberleutnant Eyer, Oberleutnant Wettstein, and Oberleutnant Teumer. Oberleutnant Wettstein later assumed command of 6 Staffel (after reorganization) and led this unit up until the end of the war. Oberleutnant Teumer became Kapitän of 7 Staffel and was presented with the Knight's Cross on 19 August 1944 after 76 kills. As a Hauptmann with "Kommando Nowotny", Teumer was fatally injured in a crash with his Me 262 during landing on 4 October 1944 due to an engine flameout.

Russian aircraft development didn't remain in the same state as was encountered in 1941. The times of the I-16 and I-153 were long past. The MiG-3 shown here is a good example. 3,300 examples of this sleek fighter were produced. A few numbers reveal the enormous efforts put forth by the Russian air armament, particularly in the area of fighter production: beginning in 1942 6,300 Yak-7b airplanes were going to the front units. There were even 16,700 of the improved Yak-9D. 10,000 of the La-5FN were produced and even the La-7 had reached 5,700 by 1944. In addition, there were 9,400 fighters which America had delivered to the Soviet Union under the Lend-Lease agreement.

The third Kommodore of the Grünherzgeschwader, Oberstleutnant Hubertus von Bonin, fell in combat near Orsha on 15 December 1943. The Kommodore had scored a total of 77 air victories. He had been awarded the Knight's Cross on 21 December 1942 after 51 kills. His successor as the fourth Kommodore in January 1944 was Oberstleutnant Anton Mader.

Oberstleutnant Mader came from the Reichsverteidigung (Reich Defense), where he had successfully led Jagdgeschwader 11. Approximately 25 western kills are included in his 86 victories.

Starting in 1943, a mutual "adoption" developed between members of the Grünherzgeschwader and the employees of the Thuringian "Mercedes" Büromaschinen-Werk in Zella-Mehlis. Visits by the Grünherz fighters in Thuringia formed close ties. (Photo) Direktor Anschütz welcomes his guests.

On 20 January 1944 the following pilots spent time in Zella-Mehlis: (from right) Prof. Haase, Hauptmann Nowotny, former Kommodore Oberst Trautloft, Major "Seppl" Seiler and Geschwaderadjutant Hauptmann Otto Kath.

As early as the spring of 1943, Oak Leaves wearer Hauptmann Stotz visited the factory with a delegation.

After the death of Hauptmann Jung Major Rudorffer took over as commander of II Gruppe on 1 August 1943. Erich Rudorffer had previously been Kapitän of 6 Staffel of Jagdgeschwader 2 in the West. The photo shows Major Rudorffer (far left) with his Staffelkapitäne in Karachev.

Hauptmann Nowotny and Unteroffizier Richter following Nowotny's last two kills on the Eastern Front. 255 Russian aircraft had fallen to his guns by 5 November 1943. After 250 victories the 22-year old Hauptmann was awarded the "Diamonds." Nowotny was given command of Jagdgeschwader 101 in Paux, southern France. The leadership of I Gruppe was transferred to Hauptmann Horst Ademeit in January 1944.

Leutnant Emil Lang was able to shoot down 18 Russian planes over Kiev at the end of October 1943 in successive sorties. The upper photo shows "Bully" Lang sitting in his aircraft after his 15th kill. The Fw 190 is being refuelled and rearmed. After his last combat sortie of the day 18 of the enemy had been knocked from the skies by the Bavarian. On 22 November 1943 Lang was awarded the Knight's Cross after his 119th air victory. While a Hauptmann and Kommandeur of II Gruppe/JG 26 in the West, "Bully" Lang fell to his death on 3 September 1944 in combat with Thunderbolts.

The lower photo shows the title cover of the Berliner Illustrierte Zeitung from 13 January 1944; the "black men" carry the victor on their shoulders.

Leutnant Heinz Wernicke (far right) and Leutnant Albin Wolf (second from right) on the wing of an Fw 190. Leutnant Wolf assumed command of 6 Staffel from Horst Ademeit on 4 February 1944.

6 Staffel, which was taken over by Leutnant Heinz Sterr following the death of Leutnant Wolf. From left to right: Unteroffizier Becker, ?, Feldwebel Lehmann, Leutnant Sterr, Feldwebel Lüneburg, Oberfähnrich Haase, Leutnant Resch, and Leutnant Hoffmann (RK 28 January 1945 posthumous).

The Kommandeur of I Gruppe, Hauptmann Ademeit, was presented the Oak Leaves on 2 March 1944 after 120 victories. This photo may have been taken in July 1944. It shows (from left to right): Kommodore Oberstleutnant Mader, Hauptmann Ademeit, Geschwaderadjutant Lock, and Hauptmann Rugenstein.

The Ergänzungsstaffel, established in October 1940 under Oberleutnant Zilken in Bergen (Holland), found itself in Cazaux, France in January of 1941. Standing in front of a Bf 109E are (from left to right): Leutnant Frenzel-Beyme, a fighter instructor in the E-Staffel, Oberleutnant von Werden and the Staffelkapitän of the E-Staffel, Oberleutnant Eggers.

Fähnriche of the E-Staffel in Cazaux, 16 February 1941. Recognizable are: Hannig (far left), Heyer (center, waving), and Hünerfeld (center, front).

The ground crew use their spare time to go fishing in the Atlantic.

Three young pilots from the E-Staffel on a tour of Paris (from left to right): Döblele, Kretschmer, and Zander.

Windau (Ventspils), August 1941. From here the young pilots flew their first operations in the Eastern campaign. Initially, these consisted of air observation of the Baltic Sea, covering German shipping convoys to Riga, later to include free ranging fighter sweeps over the Kronstadt Bay and attacking Russian supply columns in the Leningrad area.

"Country Idyll" at the airfield in Windau.

During the first Russian winter the E-Staffel was based in Siverskaya and flew combat operations from here. Beneath the pilot's cockpit can be seen the coat-of-arms for the E-Staffel to good effect.

Despite being seriously damaged by flak over the Neva, this pilot managed to bring his Bf 109 safely back to Siverskaya. On 9 March 1942 the E-Staffel was disbanded, with personnel and aircraft being assigned to other Staffeln of the Geschwader. The young pilots had successfully completed their baptism of fire, scoring 51 kills in the process.

After disbandment, a newly established Ergänzungsjagdgeschwader in the rear area assumed training responsibilities of additional replacement pilots for all fighter units. It contained an Ergänzungsgruppe Ost and West, and Jagdgeschwader 54 provided flight instructors for these Gruppen. These were proven front-line fighter pilots who could pass their experience and talents on to the younger fighter pilots. Leutnant Otto Kittel was also among those trainers in Ergänzungsgruppe Ost in Biarritz during the winter of 1943/1944.

Here in Biarritz a young pilot familiarizes himself with the strengths of the Focke-Wulf 190.

Oberst Trautloft, Inspekteur der Tagjäger in the Stab of the Generals der Jagdflieger, visits the E-Gruppe Ost in Biarritz. Leutnant Kittel is given a warm greeting by his former Kommodore. On the right is the Kommodore of the Ergänzungsgeschwader, Major Werner Andres.

Maintenance personnel seen adjusting the internal guns of an Fw 190 in Dorpat.

Oberfeldwebel Missner also belonged to Ergänzungsgruppe Ost as a fighter instructor. As a pilot in I Gruppe in the East he had scored 82 victories. Helmut Missner died in combat on 12 September 1944 in Sagan. He was posthumously awarded the Knight's Cross for his successes on 10 October 1944.

As at the fighter schools, theoretical instruction on the "Revi" (REflexVIsier) gunsights and aircraft models was also carried out at the E-Gruppen.

Aircraft recognition was just as much a part of the instruction as sighting and estimating the right amount of deflection. Four proven front-line flyers from JG 54, now fighter instructors in Liegnitz. From left to right: Oberfeldwebel Kroschinski and Brill, Feldwebel Raupach, and Unteroffizier Luer.

Showing the old ties to the Geschwader, the "Green Heart" carries the three coats-of-arms of the Gruppen, with its members in a different order this time. From left to right: Raupach, Kroschinski, Brill, and Luer.

The larger flying formations employed during the Reichsverteidigung played a large part of the training for the fighter pilots. Conditions were different in the West than in the East. In Liegnitz, 2 Staffel of the E-Gruppe practiced formation flying, which was a prerequisite for success against large bomber formations.

Takeoff in Rotte formation, no easy task for the young fighter pilots.

30 September 1944, Sagan. Leutnant Rudi Rademacher is awarded the Knight's Cross by Oberst Trautloft after 95 aerial victories. From the left is Oberst Trautloft, Hauptmann Otto Kath, Oberleutnant Udo Hünerfeld and Hauptmann Maierl.

Oberst Trautloft inspects the front row of the Gruppe. Rademacher was severely injured on 18 September 1944 during an attack on an American heavy bomber formation. From January 1945 Rademacher flew in JG 7 and was numbered among the most successful pilots with the Me 262.

Operations of II Gruppe in Finland.

Italian crews flew ground crew to Immola, Finland in their Savoia 81s; the men here are from 4 Staffel.

Pilots of 5 Staffel prior to the flight to Finland. From left to right: Unteroffizier Asche, Leutnant Thyben, Oberleutnant Schilling (Staffel leader), Leutnant Arnecke, Unteroffizier Bernd, Feldwebel Mischalla, Obergefreiter Fädrich, and in the window, Unteroffizier Koller. Fädrich died on 16 June 1944 when his plane flipped over during an interim landing in Helsinki.

The Staffeln were based at airfields such as Helsinki, Petäjarvi and Immola, and for the duration of their operations were subordinate to Gefechtsverband Kuhlmey.

Taking off on a combat mission from Petseri, Leutnant Wolf – Kapitän of 6 Staffel – scored the 7,000th kill for the Grünherzgeschwader. For Wolf himself, this was his 135th victory.

Unbelievable: this photo was taken in Immola around 11 p.m. Maintenance crew of 5 Staffel on their way to the barracks.

A Focke-Wulf 190 A-6 at the Immola dispersal area.

Scrapbook photo with the Finnish squadron commander, Captain Krukunen, in Turku. From left to right: Leutnant Tegtmeier (RK 28 March 1944 with 99 kills), Captain Kurkunen, Oberleutnant Jung (Finnish liaison officer), Oberleutnant zur See Abraham, Oberleutnant Wettstein, and Leutnant Rademacher.

Major Rudorffer, sitting on the vehicle, leaves Finland with his II Gruppe.

The Bf 109 of the Kommandeur of III Gruppe, Major Seiler, parked in front of the camouflaged flight control center in Oldenburg. "Pari-Pari" proudly guards his master's heavily armed airplane.

Hein Wübke was well-known throughout the entire Geschwader for his dry sense of humor. In Vendeville, while Kapitän of 7 Staffel, he arranged a concert in the town square. According to spectators, with the exception of the accordion player, not a single one of the "musicians" had the slightest clue how to play his instrument. The effect was said to have been disastrous!

Hauptmann Bob (left), Kapitän of 9 Staffel, helps to coax a few more notes from the instrument.

Hauptmann Fink (center) led 8 Staffel. A communal game of skat drives away the inner anxiety while sitting on alert. The photo shows Oberleutnant Brock, Hauptmann Fink, and the Unteroffiziere Wulfers and Weber.

Setting out from Oldenburg, III Gruppe was used to protect the German coast and interior. Accordingly, life jackets and air-sea rescue equipment were part of the basic flying ensemble for each pilot.

Oberst Günther Lützow pays a visit to the Gruppe in Vendeville in April 1943. From left to right: Gäth, Seiler, Lützow, and Lederer.

Major "Seppl" Seiler was once again transferred to the Eastern Front on 15 April 1943, where he was put in charge of I Gruppe. Here, he says goodbye to the men of III Gruppe in front of the control tower. The man shaking his hand is Hauptmann Fink.

The new Kommandeur of III Gruppe is Hauptmann Siegfried Schnell. Oberst Trautloft is seen in conversation with Schnell. On the right is Major Seiler.

A group photo in front of the mess in Oldenburg. From left to right: Neumann, Seiler, Terp, Klemm, Schnell, ?, an inspector, Rugenstein, hidden ?, half-hidden Patzak, and Wübke.

In the spring of 1943 Oberfeldwebel Zweigert was reassigned from 5 Staffel to 9 Staffel in the West. After 54 air victories, he was awarded the Knight's Cross on 22 January 1943. The photo includes Oberfeldwebel Zweigert (second from right) and Hauptmann Bob (in the center).

4 Staffel under Oberleutnant Graf von Matuschka was based in Nordholz, German Bight in May of 1943.

From 23 June to 14 August 1943 the three Staffeln of the Gruppe were based at Schipol, Arnhem and Deelen. Here in Deelen Oberst Lützow visits the Gruppe once again.

Oberst Mader, in 1943 Kommodore of JG 11, and Oberst Trautloft also pay a visit to Hauptmann Schnell's Gruppe. Oberst Mader is seen in conversation with pilots of 8 and 9 Staffel.

Günther Fink, Kapitän of 8 Staffel, failed to return from a sortie over the North Sea on 15 May 1943. Fink, a successful fighter pilot and exemplary officer, had a total of 56 kills to his credit. 8 Staffel was now commanded by Oberleutnant Patzak, who led it until his death in February of 1944. The photo shows (from left to right): Oberleutnant Brock, Oberleutnant Patzak, Leutnant Bock, and Oberfeldwebel Müller.

On 15 May 1943 Leutnant Friedrich Rupp (left), an old, experienced pilot from 7 Staffel, also fell southwest of Heligoland. The Knight's Cross had been presented to Rupp on 24 January 1943 after 52 victories. Two four-engine bombers fell to his guns in the West. This successful pilot found his final resting place in Wehr am Rhein, his hometown in Baden-Württemburg (below).

Hauptmann Siegfried Schnell was transferred to the Eastern Front on 1 February 1944 as commander of IV/JG 54 in exchange for Hauptmann Sinner. After being wounded in a dogfight, Sinner was forced to relinquish his command of III Gruppe to Hauptmann Werner Schroer on 14 March 1944. Hauptmann Schroer is second from right in the picture, seen in April 1944 at the Lüneburg airfield. In the background is Generalmajor Max Ibel (second from left).

Leutnant Eugen-Ludwig Zweigert assumed command of the orphaned 8 Staffel in February. Leutnant Zweigert (second from left) is seen conversing with Major Hermann Graf and Oberleutnant Klemm (Kapitän of 7 Staffel, far right). Zweigert fell on 8 June 1944 over Normandy as an Oberleutnant with 69 victories.

Leutnant Reinhold, too, was killed on 24 May 1944 when his plane flipped over during an emergency landing. He scored 60 kills in Russia and shot down another four heavy bombers in the West. This courageous flyer was posthumously awarded the Knight's Cross on 28 January 1945.

Hauptmann "Bully" Lang was reassigned from the Grünherzgeschwader on 25 July 1944 to become Kommandeur of II Gruppe of Jagdgeschwader 26. With 144 victories, he was awarded the Oak Leaves on 11 April 1944. Emil Lang fell on 3 September 1944 in combat with Thunderbolts after having scored another 25 kills in the West.

In July of 1944 Hauptmann Werner Schroer was transferred to the Verbandsführerschule in Königsberg. Hauptmann Robert Weiss filled his place as Kommandeur of III/JG 54. This photo shows "Bazi" Weiss (right front) at the Gruppe command post in Villacoublay, together with Red Cross nurses from the Luftwaffe hospital in Paris-Clichy.

Hauptmann Weiss with two successful pilots at the Villacoublay South airbase. "Bazi" Weiss led III Gruppe during the costly battles on the invasion front and during the Reichsverteidigung. He himself perished with 121 victories on 29 December 1944 in combat with large Spitfire formations in the area of Lingen/Ems. Weiss was posthumously awarded the Oak Leaves.

A IV Gruppe of the Grünherzgeschwader was established in July of 1943 by Hauptmann Erich Rudorffer in Jesau near Königsberg. But just five days later Hauptmann Rudi Sinner was put in charge of the Gruppe, since Rudorffer was ordered to assume command of the orphaned II Gruppe on the Eastern Front. Initially, IV Gruppe fought in the northern sector of the Eastern Front until being transferred to the airbases at Idritsa, Dno, Pleskau and Dorpat.

The "black men" at work on the aircraft of Leutnant Thielen in Dorpat.

Scramble by Unteroffizier Schneiker, 12 Staffel, in Dorpat.

Four jovial pilots of 12 Staffel in Dorpat. From left to right: Unteroffizier Schneiker, Leutnant Thielen, Oberfähnrich Bauer, and Leutnant Hartrampf.

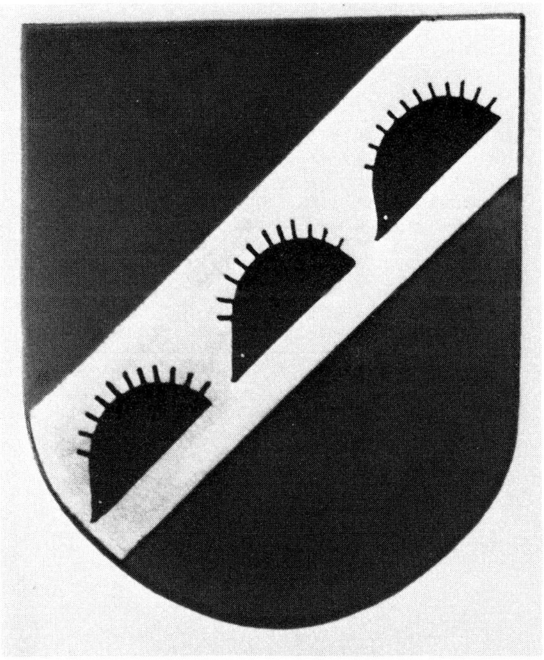

This coat-of-arms was carried by the aircraft of IV Gruppe under Hauptmann Sinner. It was the coat-of-arms of the Prince of Savoy and carried three hedgehogs on a white band with a red background.

Hauptmann Rudi Sinner, the second Kommandeur of IV Gruppe. He came from JG 27, the renowned Desert Geschwader from Africa. He developed his great flying and organizational talents while Kommandeur of a Gruppe in JG 7. With the Me 262 he scored some of the last victories over the Reich territory.

Christmas 1943 in Dno. The Kommandeur with his staff NCOs. On the far left is an assemblyman from Daimler-Benz. The Spiess of the Stabskompanie is third from left, then Hauptmann Sinner and Leutnant Gröne (intelligence officer).

Hauptmann Sinner's successor in February 1944 after his transfer to III Gruppe was Hauptmann Siegfried Schnell. Schnell was killed in combat not long after, on 25 February. The Gruppe was then temporarily led by Hauptmann Gerhard Koall, whose 12 Staffel was taken over by Hauptmann "Hein" Wübke. At the end of May 1944 the decimated Gruppe transferred via Landau (Isar) to Illesheim, where they converted to the Fw 190 A-8. Here, under the command of Major Wolfgang Späte, the Gruppe underwent a virtual reorganization. Major Späte is to the right in the photo, while on the far left is Oberleutnant Erwin Leykauf. Third from left is Oberleutnant Rudolf Klemm, then Oberleutnant Gröne.

By now IV Gruppe fell in line with Geschwader tradition and took as its coat-of-arms that of the city of Königsberg, as a tribute to the place of the unit's birth. The stylized coat-of-arms of Königsberg in East Prussia is seen here on the engine housing.

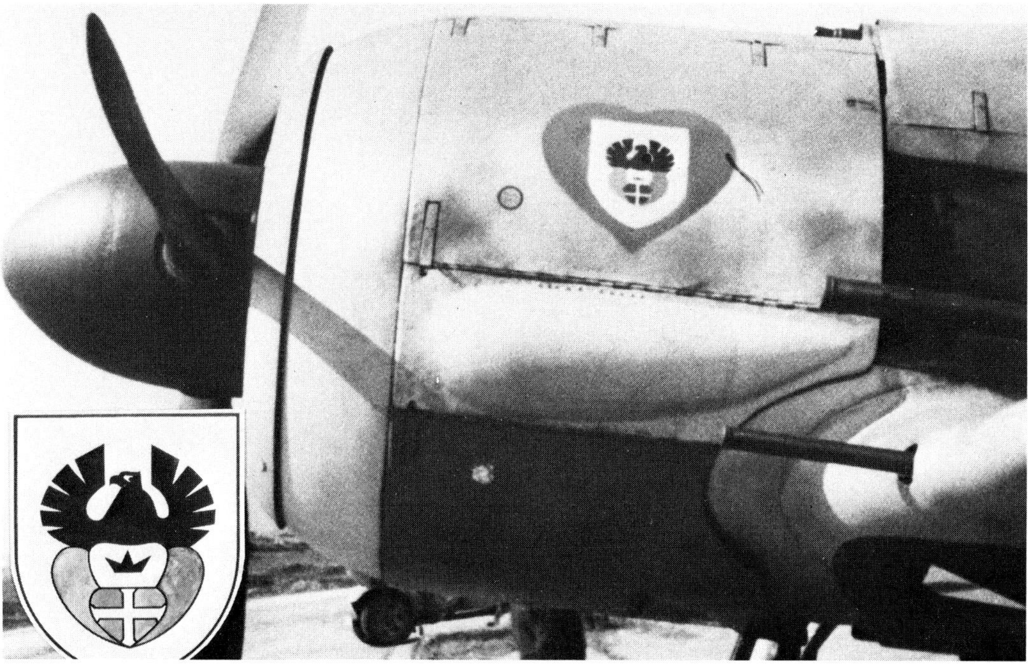

In addition to reequipping with the Fw 190 A-8 the Gruppe was also reinforced with a fourth Staffel. The maintenance personnel very quickly became familiar with the Focke-Wulf. This photo shows maintenance being carried out on a plane wearing the Gruppe's symbol.

The Gruppe suffered bitter losses in Staffelkapitäne and pilots, constantly being shuttled back and forth from East to West as a "flying fire brigade." From 1 November 1944 Leutnant Karl Brill (left) commanded 13 Staffel and after Oberleutnant Sterr was killed in action Leutnant Paul Brandt took over 16 Staffel. Brandt, a recipient of the Knight's Cross, fell to his death on 24 December 1944 near Münster, Westphalia. Four heavy bombers were among his 34 aerial victories.

During October and November of 1944 15 Staffel under Staffelkapitän Leutnant Resch operated out of Möritz, flying costly missions in defense of the Reich. From left to right: a mechanic, Gefreiter Stackhof, Oberfeldwebel Schmeink, Feldwebel Bitze, Leutnant Resch, Oberfeldwebel Schultz, Oberfeldwebel Timm, Unteroffizier Walter, Gefreiter Bechert, and Feldwebel Styx.

Hauptmann Rudolf Klemm took over the Gruppe in mid-October 1944. Major Späte became Kommodore of JG 400, which was equipped with the Me 163 "Kraftei" (lit. "Powered Egg"). Hauptmann Klemm was awarded the Knight's Cross on 18 November after his 40th kill. Altogether he bested 42 enemy planes, including 16 four-engined bombers.

On 14 January 1945 the remains of IV Gruppe under the command of the Kapitän of 15 Staffel, Leutnant Resch, flew their last mission from Voerde airbase. During an attack on heavy bomber formations, the numerically superior American fighters practically gutted the Gruppe. Only two pilots returned; 14 planes were shot down. In February the IV Gruppe was disbanded.

A second "reestablishment" of IV Gruppe in the spring of 1945 was only a renaming of II Gruppe of Zerstörergeschwader 76. The unit converted from Me 410s to Fw 190s in Grossenhain. Here in Grossenhain Oberstleutnant Hrabak, the fifth Kommodore of JG 54 from October 1944, inspects the Gruppe. However, at no time was the Gruppe ever directly subordinate to the Grünherzgeschwader. Its operational orders came from the Jagddivision in Bad Saarow. The Gruppe suffered its most severe losses during a combined attack with bombs on the Oder bridges and positions in the area of Göritz-Lebus. More than 15 of the clumsy planes, loaded with 250 kg bombs, were shot down by Mustangs. The photos show the new IV Gruppe being accepted by Oberstleutnant Hrabak in Grossenhain. To the right next to Hrabak is the Kommandeur of the Gruppe, Hauptmann Karl Fritz Schlossstein.

Starting in June of 1944, beneath the massive pressure of the Russian summer offensive, units of Heeresgruppe Nord gradually and in an organized fashion began pulling back via Riga into the region of Courland. By maintaining constant operations the Grünherz fighters fought off attacks by the marauding Soviet air force. This photo was taken in the summer of 1944 at the airfield in Skirotava. On the far left is Oberleutnant Otto Kittel and his wingman, Feldwebel Ulrich Wernitz (fourth from right).

Riga, 15 August 1944. Oberleutnant Kittel (center) after the 100th victory of 3 Staffel. Otto Kittel was presented the Swords to the Knight's Cross on 25 November 1944 for his 230 victories. He fell in combat on 14 February 1945 after 267 kills.

By mounting surprise attacks the Russian air force attempted to strike the German fighter bases and destroy the hated enemy. On 18 November 1944, II Gruppe looked to be in a rather chaotic state following an attack by 50 Pe-2 bombers. These men of the Kraftfahrzug (roughly, "motor pool") attempt to quench the flames.

After bailing out, this Russian major was captured and interrogated near the Riga-Skirotava airfield. In the photo from right to left are: Hauptmann Schaffrin (Chief of the Stabskompanie), Hauptmann Eisenach, Kommandeur of I Gruppe, Oberfeldwebel Hesse (Stabsschwarm), a translator from the Army, the Russian major.

Leutnant Heinz Wernicke, Kapitän of 1 Staffel, was presented the Knight's Cross by Generaloberst Pflugbeil on 30 September 1944 after 112 air victories. Wernicke was rammed by his own wingman on 27 December 1944 and plummeted to his death.

7 Staffel under Leutnant Thyben scored its 1000th kill over the Courland pocket.

Leutnant Schulz reports the 100th victory of the Staffel to the commanding officer of the newly established 6 Staffel, Hauptmann Wettstein.

Hauptmann Franz Eisenach, Kommandeur of I Gruppe, takes the post-mission report in Libau.

Leutnant Gerhard Thyben, Kapitän of 7 Staffel, is presented the Knight's Cross by Generaloberst Pflugbeil in Libau-North. Gerhard Thyben is far right; Generaloberst Pflugbeil is in discussion with pilots of 7 Staffel.

Santa Claus (Feldwebel Fritz Hangebrauk) arrives in his Fw 190 at Libau-North in the Courland pocket. A welcome guest at 7 Staffel.

The "Inspekteur der Tagjäger", Hannes Trautloft, visits the Grünherz fighters in the Courland pocket. Trautloft is seen in conversation with pilots of 7 Staffel. On the far right is the fifth and last Kommodore of JG 54, Hrabak, and Leutnant Thyben.

The last Christmas of the war in the Courland pocket. Leutnant Thyben and Unteroffizier Walter Pahl in the bunker at the Libau-North airbase.

Beginning of January 1945 – four flyers of 6 Staffel. In the Fw 190 is Oberfeldwebel Mahlau (KIA), from left: Feldwebel Toni Meissner, Oberfähnrich Schreiber, Leutnant Norbert Hannig and two mechanics, the Obergefreiten Plomer and Bronner.

In February of 1945 Major Rudorffer was replaced as Kommandeur of II Gruppe, transferring to Jagdgeschwader 7. The new Kommandeur of II/JG 54 was Hauptmann Herbert Findeisen. The successful reconnaissance pilot had only been a fighter pilot since the end of 1944. He was awarded the Knight's Cross after 36 kills while a recon pilot. Findeisen died in May of 1963 in an automobile accident. From left to right: Pflugbeil, Rudorffer, Hrabak, and Findeisen.

Dispersal area of 6 Staffel in Libau-North. An Fw 190 is kept ready for operations during a snowstorm.

Leutnant Schleinhege and Leutnant Thyben seen while leaving the Gruppe command post.

February 1945 – Hauptmann Findeisen with three of his Staffelkapitäne in the Gruppe's command post in Libau. From left to right: Leutnant Thyben (7 Staffel), Hauptmann Findeisen, Leutnant Schleinhege (8 Staffel, RK 19 February 1945), Leutnant Wöhnert (5 Staffel, RK 6 December 1944).

Pilots of the "new 6 Staffel" in front of the bunker in Libau eating stew.

Hauptmann Wettstein's indominable 6 Staffel with several aircraft mechanics in front of the bunker.

On 25 February 1945 Unteroffizier Albrecht Licht was awarded the Iron Cross 1st Class. From left to right: unknown Unteroffizier, Hauptmann Wettstein, Unteroffizier "Bobby" Moser with dachshund "Löwe", Oberfähnrich Schreiber, Unteroffizier Licht, Unteroffizier Hammerschmidt, Leutnant Hannig, Oberfeldwebel Mahlau (KIA), Gefreiter Handke (KIA).

Leutnant Hugo Broch, a pilot in 8 Staffel, was presented the Knight's Cross by Generaloberst Pflugbeil on 12 March 1945 at the Cirava airbase in Courland. Leutnant Broch is seen reviewing the front column of the Staffel with Generaloberst Pflugbeil.

Generaloberst Pflugbeil in conversation with Leutnant Broch and the Kapitän of 8 Staffel, Leutnant Schleinhege.

Concerned expressions: Leutnant Schleinhege injured his hand on the opener of a bottle of sekt.

The Grünherz fighters in the Courland pocket also flew escort for these unusual birds. These were Ju 52s tasked with clearing the supply routes for German transport shipping. By generating an electromagnetic field it was possible to detonate both drift and anchor mines.

Unteroffizier Albrecht Licht in his Fw 190 A-8, which carries the tactical number "yellow 8", in March 1945.

In March of 1945 Leutnant Norbert Hannig, together with his Schwarm, sunk a Russian torpedo boat. Another craft was set afire and also sank later. The four successful pilots, from left to right: Feldwebel Edgar Meschkat, Unteroffizier Albrecht Licht, Leutnant Norbert Hannig, and Unteroffizier Kohler.

Oberleutnant Thyben scored a total of 157 victories in the air. On 8 April 1945 he was awarded the Oak Leaves to the Knight's Cross. During his flight out of the Courland pocket on 8 May 1945, Thyben scored the last kill of the Grünherzgeschwader – with two of the "black men" stowed inside his fuselage.

Last briefing, in front of the bunker in Libau. From the left are Kommodore Hrabak, Hauptmann Wettstein, Hauptmann Findeisen, and Generaloberst Pflugbeil.

Three days before the capitulation. Armorers of 7 Staffel in the Courland pocket.

The ground personnel were carried to Flensburg, transported by naval ships, in transport aircraft, and even in the units' own Fw 190 fighters. Two to three of the "black men" were "stashed" in the cockpit and fuselage of the aircraft. Heino Cordes, Arthur Lotz and Hans Gött were the last pilots to leave the pocket with their aircraft.

Due to a fuel shortage, pilot Karl-Heinz Ramm and his crew chief, Obergefreiter Hans Günther, belly landed in Denmark on 8 May 1945.

In Flensburg, the Fw 190 crews were received by British soldiers. The reception was fair; initially no disarmament even took place. In the background can be seen the Fw 190s flown out of Courland.

The war is over; officers of the Grünherzgeschwader in Odderage in British internment, summer 1945. From left to right: Rugenstein, Eberwein, Eisenach, Schultz, Findeisen, Lock, and Hrabak.

Humor bursts forth once again! Herbert Findeisen in Odderade.

After the war the former Grünherz fighters met at regular intervals. Now the wives and often the children came. Externally, nearly all of the Grünherz fighters have changed over the course of the years, yet the spirit binding them has developed into a solid brotherhood. Here and there one spirit becomes silent, then the remaining grow even closer together. And may it always be so!

This photo was taken during a Geschwader convention in Fürstenfeldbruck. Hans-Joachim Kroschinski, blinded during the war, probes a T-33. It's a photograph which has a profound effect upon the viewer. At the same time, it is also a manifestation of the deep alliance with all those who, in their younger years, found themselves struck down by the fate of the horrible war. They remain a living brotherhood, also tied to those who were not able to experience peacetime.

In a ceremony on 26 November 1982 Jagdgeschwader 34 in Memmingen formally assumed the heraldic rights to the former Jagdgeschwader 54 "Grünherz."

Former Kommodore Hannes Trautloft addresses the guests present. Among these are (from left to right): Generalmajor a.D. Hrabak, Generalleutnant a.D. Rall, Minister a.D. Georg Leber, and the Komodore of Jabo Geschwader 34, Oberst Hammerstein.

Major Detlef Scharf, Staffelkapitän of 1 Staffel, Jagdbombergeschwader 34, signs the certificate accepting the legacy of the Grünherzgeschwader.

Laying a wreath at the memorial to the dead of the Grünherzgeschwader and to the young pilots of the Jagdbombergeschwader 34 who gave their lives during the course of their duties.

Former Kommodore Trautloft presents a model of an Bf 109 to the Traditionsstaffel. On the left are Hannes Trautloft and the Staffelkapitän, Major Scharf. In the background are Starfighter pilots of the Traditionsstaffel.

1 Staffel accepts the "Grünherz" banner.

"Old" and "new" Grünherz fighters during the transfer of the banner.

Two generations in front of a Lockheed F-104 Starfighter carrying the "Grünherz" coat-of-arms in Memmingen. From left to right: Major Scharf, Kapitän of 1 Staffel Jagdbombergeschwader 34, Hannes Trautloft, former Kommodore of JG 54 "Grünherz", Oberst Hammerstein, Kommodore of Jagdbombergeschwader 34.

Former "Grünherz" fighters of JG 54 – forty years on! From right to left: Schmoller-Haldy, Seliger, Kath, von Obernitz, Mettig, Hrabak, Trautloft, Treiber, Oberst Hammerstein, and Major Scharf.

Group photo of former "Grünherz" fighter pilots and pilots of 1 Staffel in front of a Tornado wearing the "Grünherz" coat-of-arms.

Appendix

Commanding Officers of Jagdgeschwader 54 "Grünherz"

The Kommodore:

1. Major Martin Mettig	2 February 1940 to 25 August 1940
2. Oberst Hannes Trautloft	25 August 1940 to 5 July 1943
3. Major Hubertus von Bonin	6 July 1943 until his death in combat on 15 December 1943
4. Oberstleutnant Anton Mader	28 January 1944 to September 1944
5. Oberst Dieter Hrabak	1 October 1944 until war's end in May 1945

The Kommandeure of I JG 54

1. Major von Cramon	09/15/1939 – 12/27/1939
2. Hauptmann von Bonin	12/28/1939 – 07/01/1941
3. Hauptmann von Selle	07/02/1941 – 12/20/1941
4. Hauptmann Eckerle	12/20/1941 – 02/14/1942
5. Hauptmann Philipp	02/17/1942 – 04/01/1943
6. Major Seiler	04/15/1943 – 07/06/1943
7. Major Homuth	08/01/1943 – 08/03/1943
8. Hauptmann Nowotny	08/10/1943 – 02/04/1944
9. Hauptmann Ademeit	02/04/1944 – 08/08/1944
10. Hauptmann Eisenach	08/09/1944 – war's end

The Kommandeure of II/JG 54

1. Hauptmann von Müller-Riensburg	1938
2. Major Blumensaat	01/10/1940 – 02/05/1940
3. Major Kraut	03/05/1940 – 07/10/1940
4. Hauptmann Winterer	07/11/1940 – 08/14/1940
5. Hauptmann/Major Hrabak	08/26/1940 – 10/27/1942
6. Hauptmann/Major Hahn	11/19/1942 – 02/21/1943
7. Hauptmann Jung	02/21/1943 – 07/30/1943
8. Hauptmann Rudorffer	08/01/1943 – February 1945
9. Hauptmann Findeisen	February 1945 – war's end

The Kommandeure of III/JG 54

1. Major Mettig	07/15/1939 – 02/02/1940
2. Hauptmann Ultsch	02/03/1940 – 09/05/1940
3. Oberleutnant Scholz*	09/06/1940 – 11/04/1940
4. Hauptmann Lignitz	11/04/1940 – 09/30/1940
5. Hauptmann Seiler	10/01/1940 – 04/15/1940
6. Hauptmann Schnell	May 1943 – 02/01/1944
7. Oberleutnant Patzak*	
8. Hauptmann Klemm*	
9. Hauptmann Sinner	March 1944 – 03/10/1944
10. Hauptmann Schroer	03/14/1944 – 07/20/1944
11. Hauptmann Weiss	07/21/1944 – 12/29/1944
12. Oberleutnant Dortenmann*	
13. Oberleutnant Heilmann*	
14. Hauptmann/Major Klemm	February 1945 to 04/17/1945 (Gruppe disbanded)

The Kommandeure of IV/JG 54

1. Hauptmann Rudorffer	Formation – 07/30/1943
2. Hauptmann Sinner	07/30/1943 – February 1944
3. Hauptmann Schnell	02/11/1944 – 02/25/1944
4. Hauptmann Koall*	March 1944 – May 1944
5. Hauptmann/Major Späte	May 1944 – 09/30/1944
6. Hauptmann Klemm	10/01/1944 until disbandment in February of 1945

* temporary

Recipients of the Knight's Cross in Jagdgeschwader 54 "Grünherz"

Oak Leaves with Swords and Diamonds to the Knight's Cross of the Iron Cross:

Nowotny, Walter*

Oak Leaves with Swords to the Knight's Cross of the Iron Cross

Kittel, Otto*
Ostermann, Hellmuth*
Philipp, Hans*
Rudorffer, Erich
Schroer, Werner*

Oak Leaves to the Knight's Cross of the Iron Cross

Ademeit, Horst*
Beisswenger, Hans*
Eckerle, Franz*
Hahn, Hans*
Hannig, Horst*
Hrabak, Dietrich
Lang, Emil*
Schnell, Siegfried*
Seiler, Reinhard
Späte, Wolfgang
Stotz, Max*
Thyben, Gerhard
Weiss, Robert*
Wolf, Albin*

Knight's Cross to the Iron Cross

Bob, Hans-Ekkehard
von Bonin, Hubertus*
Brandt, Paul*
Broch, Hugo
Broennle, Herbert*
Döbele, Anton*
Dortenmann, Hans*
Eisenach, Franz
Findeisen, Herbert*
Fink, Günther*
Götz, Hans*
Grollmus, Helmut*
Gross, Alfred*
Heyer, Hans-Joachim*
Hirschfeld, Ernst-Erich*
Hoffmann, Reinhold*
Homuth, Gerhard*
Jung, Heinrich*
Kempf, Karl*
Klemm, Rudolf
Koall, Gerhard*
Kroschinski, Hans-Joachim
Lange, Heinz
Lignitz, Arnold*
Loos, Gerhard*
Mader, Anton
Missner, Helmut*
Mütherich, Hubert*
Philipp, Wilhelm
Pöss, Josef*
Rademacher, Rudolf*
Rupp, Friedrich*
Sattig, Karl*
Scheel, Günther*
Schilling, Wilhelm
Schleinhege, Hermann
Schnörrer, Karl*
Seiffert, Heinz*
Siegler, Peter*
Sterr, Heinrich*
Tegtmeier, Fritz
Teumer, Alfred*
Trautloft, Hannes*
Wandel, Joachim*
Wernicke, Heinz*
Wernitz, Ulrich
Wöhnert, Ulrich*
Zweigert, Eugen*

*deceased at time of publication in original German (1985)